Tips on Making Greeting Cards

Bill Gray
and
Jane Van Milligen

 DESIGN PRESS

Other books in the Tips Series:
Studio Tips
More Studio Tips
Lettering Tips
Tips On Type
Calligraphy Tips

First Edition, Third Printing
Copyright © 1991 by Jane Van Milligen
and Karen Gray.
Printed in the United States of America
Designed by Jane Van Milligen

Design Press offers posters and
The Cropper, a device for cropping
artwork, for sale. For information,
contact Mail-order Department.
Design Press books are available
at special discounts for bulk pur-
chases for sale promotions, fund
raisers, or premiums. For details
contact Special Sales Manager.
Questions regarding the content of
the book should be addressed to:
Design Press
11 West 19th Street
New York, NY 10011

Design Press books are published
by Design Press an imprint of TAB
Books. TAB Books is a division of
McGraw-Hill, Inc. The Design
Press logo is a trademark of TAB
Books.

Library of Congress Cataloging-in-
Publication Data
GRAY, BILL
    TIPS ON GREETING CARD DESIGN / BILL GRAY
    AND JANE VAN MILLIGEN
        p. cm.
    INCLUDES INDEX
    ISBN 0-8306-0595-9
    1. GREETING CARDS--DESIGN.
        I. VAN MILLIGEN, JANE. II. TITLE.
NC 1860.G64 1991
741.6'84 -- dc20   90-21632
                                    CIP

Dedicated to the memory of Bill Gray –
he will be missed for many years to come.

Acknowledgments

Many thanks to Timothy and Karen Gray. Thanks also to James Van Milligen and Lisabeth Sample: without them this book would never have been realized.

Bill Gray began this book, the sixth in his Tips Series, and was working on it when he died unexpectedly in October, 1989. His son and his publisher approached me and asked if I would pick up where Bill left off. I trust this was because we had been friends, had a similar approach to research and teaching, and had discussed working on this book together. It has been an honor and a privilege to continue Bill's work.

Preface

Whether you want to mass-produce cards or make each card an original, to sell your work or give it as a gift, you will find this book to be a valuable reference. It offers a variety of subjects, and the directions are clear and to the point. As a result, it serves both the amateur and the professional. Because the subject of greeting cards is so vast and its state-of-the-art changes constantly, no book can cover it definitively. The purpose of this book, then, is to inspire you as well as to expand your knowledge. Use its ideas as springboards to new ideas – your own.

Contents

History of Greeting Cards

Egyptians who lived before the time of Christ were the first people known to use greeting cards, exchanging messages on scrolls to celebrate a new year. The Chinese and Romans, too, sent greetings on clay tablets, scrolls, and metal coins. The oldest existing holiday card from Europe was printed from a woodcut in Germany in 1450.

Christmas became the holiday most celebrated by written greetings. The tradition started in the early 1700s during the reign of Queen Anne in England. Children gave cards to their parents to show the progress in their penmanship. Then adults took up the custom, and greeting cards have been part of our life ever since.

Cards were mass produced for the first time on the printing press in England in the early 1800s. By mid-century, a New York merchant started the custom in the United States when he combined his Christmas greetings with a business advertisement. Louis Prang and Albert Davis developed greeting cards into an industry, widening the market to include other holidays. The Hall brothers began their company in the 1920s, and today the Hallmark Company is one of many card makers in the industry.

REPRINTED FROM THE ART AND CRAFT OF GREETING CARDS BY SUSAN EVARTS

This woodcut greeting card was printed in the Rhine Valley in Germany in 1450. It is the oldest existing holiday card from Europe.

Getting Ready

Greeting card designers use many techniques – from embossing, which creates an image raised above its background, to die-cutting, which allows mass-production of a cutout image. They use foil, glitter, and even wooden elements on their cards. A greeting card can be in the form of a postcard, or a card that folds to mail without an envelope. Greetings can be hand-delivered instead of mailed, providing an opportunity to experiment with technique, media, size, and form.

Both style and subject matter depend on the designer's taste. Nostalgia has brought back patterns as diverse as Victorian, op art, and country. Animals such as kittens, puppies, and carousel horses are popular. High-tech lifestyles have opened the field to computer graphics, which can be completely original or based upon scanned material.

Fluorescent colors are popular and are available as paint, paper, fabric, and markers. Choose what pleases you and the recipient is likely to be pleased too.

Start by defining the event the card is to commemorate and the general message it is to convey. Cards send congratulations for a new baby, new house, or new job. Cards celebrate personal events such as birthdays, anniversaries, and reunions. They also mark local or national and religious holidays. Some cards express sentiments such as "Have a safe trip," while others say "I'm sorry," or "I love you." Some greetings merely remind the recipient that the sender cares. Some cards extend an invitation; others accompany a gift, or are themselves the gift.

Once you have determined the card's message, you must decide on its tone – humorous, romantic, affectionate, ironic, informative, formal, and so on. The message may be in rhyme or free verse. You may rely on a well-known phrase or elect to use a straightforward message of your own composing.

You communicate your message

"A Pleasant greeting heals the spirit."

—WALT JONES
CONTEMPORARY WRITER

with graphic images as well as words. If the card is custom-made for a special person, use symbols — shop tools, computer screen, or chef's hat, for example — that represent him or her. Someone who does needlework might enjoy a valentine with a large needle, instead of an arrow, stuck through the heart on the cover. Inside the card could read, "You'd be a pain if it weren't for the thimble of love." A congratulatory card could consist of an acrylic mirror glued within a frame under which you write, "This is the portrait of a genius."

Experiment with papers, colors, textures, and media. A greeting card need not be the traditional folded sheet. Try cards that are booklets or ones that have pockets for little gifts. Design the card to open in an unusual way, or include a pop-up element. Sprinkle loose glitter or confetti inside the card so that it cascades out when the card is opened. Collage, dried flowers, and lace add texture and dimension to a card. If your card requires an envelope, include it in the total design. You can line an envelope with wrapping paper or decorate it with rubber stampings.

Copyrights and Credits

Design, artwork, or wording that is copyrighted cannot be used without permission of the person or organization holding the copyright. The copyright owner controls reproduction, sale, performance, display, and the making of derivatives of the original artwork.

Greeting card designers often use quotations, poems, photographs, or graphic elements made by other artists. When they do, they must determine whether the material is copyrighted because those who use protected material without permission are infringing upon the rights of the copyright owner, and they can be sued for damages.

Copyright law is complex. As a rule of thumb, works published and/or copyrighted prior to 1915 by United States authors are in public domain. This means no permission is required to use them. Any other work has probably been copyrighted, although in some cases the protection period has expired. For details on copyright law, write to Copyright Office, Library of Congress, Washington, DC 20559 and request the free "Copyright Information Kit."

To request permission to use a work, write to the copyright owner and explain how you plan to use his or her work and how many copies you would make. Many times the owner will permit your personal use without charging a fee. All borrowed works – even non-copyrighted ones – require acknowledgment of the copyright owner and/or the artist. Give credit to authors and artists by writing the information on the back of your card.

To copyright your original greeting card designs, write to the Copyright Office, or call its hotline (202-707-9100), and request copies of Form VA (for visual arts). Copyright now is for the life of the copyright owner plus 50 years. Copyrighting procedure involves sending the Copyright Office a $20 fee, two samples, and a completed application form for each card. If your card has not been reproduced, you may send photographs of each card instead of of the samples.

Be sure to add the copyright symbol ©, the year the card was made, and your name before letting it leave your studio.

(Reference: Legal Guide for the Visual Artist by Tad Crawford, Allworth Press)

© 1991 J. VAN MILLIGEN

Qui me furatur, in tribus tignis suspendatur.

This 15th-century Latin curse means roughly "Hanging will do for him who steals me."

Choosing The Words

The words on a greeting card should evoke the appropriate emotion, and communicate the sender's message quickly. Use good grammar, unless the wording is meant to be humorous. Short phrases work well on cards. An easy way to write your message in rhyme is to put new words to the meter of a familar poem or nursery rhyme. You achieve extra "punch" by altering the final line as in this example: "Roses are red; Violets are blue; You are forty, and I am ⋯ not!"

Use the word <u>you</u> to make the card personal and conversational. Find sayings from the Bible, Shakespeare, quotations or familiar poems, and anthologies such as <u>Bartlett's Familiar Quotations</u>. Be sure to credit the author and work. Get permission to use copyrighted material.

Consider making a play on words with a Christmas invitation: "You're invited to ho-ho-hors d'oeuvres." A riddle, or even a curse, can be humorous. Two examples of historic curses are shown at the tops of these two pages.

May he who mocks your age be sent /a blow upon his fundament. – 14th-century European curse

An abecedarian sentence would appeal to a scholar or writer. It contains all the letters in the alphabet – for example, "The quick brown fox jumps over the lazy dog." First, find words that use the most difficult letters (j, k, p, q, v, w, x, and z). For example: joy, kisses, piquant, love, wishes, mixed, and zest. Write down all the letters covered so far (a, d, e, g, h, i, j, k, l. m, n, o, p, q, s, t, u, v, w, x, y, z). Then list the ones remaining (b, c, f, and r), and finish the sentence to include them: "It's fact that my joy, love, zest, and wishes get mixed more by your piquant kisses." The goal is to use the fewest words, yet include every letter at least once.

You might also write a riddle. Or make the message out of letters cut from newspapers and magazines for a ransom-note look. Make the card into a booklet of coupons, redeemable for kisses, compliments, phone calls, back rubs, or whatever.

Here are some helpful reference books: <u>Writing</u> <u>Light</u> <u>Verse</u> by Richard Armour. Boston: The Writer, Inc., 1987; <u>Writing</u> <u>and</u> <u>Selling</u> <u>of</u> <u>Greeting</u> <u>Card</u> <u>Verse</u> by June Barr. Boston: The Writer, Inc., 1987; and <u>Selling</u> <u>Poetry</u>, <u>Verse</u>, <u>and</u> <u>Prose</u> by Carl Goeller. New York: Doubleday & Co., 1986.

TOOLS AND MATERIALS

You will need several tools and some basic materials to create a greeting card, now that you have some ideas. There are also a few optional tools that will make the job easier. Tools for specific techniques are listed with the technique later in the book.

Note: Before starting to work, please read "Safety Precautions" on page 132.

Basic Tools

A LIGHTBOX WILL HELP YOU SEE THROUGH SEVERAL LAYERS OF PAPER SO YOU CAN TRACE CERTAIN ELEMENTS. IF YOU USE A LIGHTBOX, ALSO MAKE TWO GUIDELINE SHEETS TO HELP YOU DO LETTERING. DRAW THE LINES 1/4" APART ON ACETATE WITH A SIZE 0 OR OO TECHNICAL PEN. USE ONE SHEET HORIZONTALLY AND ONE VERTICALLY. OVERLAP THEM ON THE LIGHTBOX TO CREATE A SQUARE GRID, OR CANT ONE AS SHOWN TO HELP YOU WITH LETTER SLANT.

Here are other helpful tools:

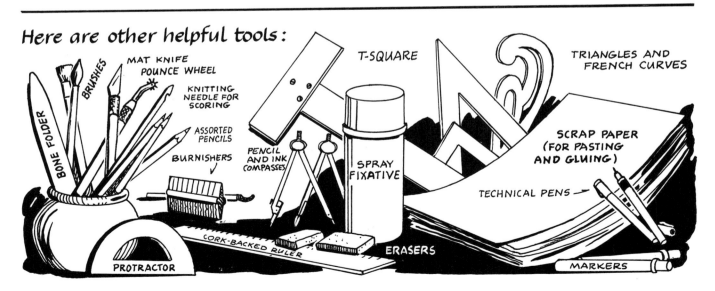

BRUSHES

MAT KNIFE
POUNCE WHEEL

KNITTING NEEDLE FOR SCORING

ASSORTED PENCILS

BONE FOLDER

BURNISHERS

PENCIL AND INK COMPASSES

PROTRACTOR

CORK-BACKED RULER

T-SQUARE

SPRAY FIXATIVE

ERASERS

TRIANGLES AND FRENCH CURVES

SCRAP PAPER (FOR PASTING AND GLUING)

TECHNICAL PENS →

MARKERS

Flat File for Storing Paper

Buy four pieces of ¼" thick foam core board 32"x40". You also will need white glue, straight pins, mat knife, yardstick, and 2" wide tape to hinge the front spacers and cover. The box made with these materials can hold paper as large as 25"x39". It has three shelves and fits under most beds. Cut the following pieces:

A AND F—TWO SHORT END PIECES, 25 ¾"X 6"

C AND D—TWO SHELF PIECES, 39 ¾"X 25 ¾"

G—ONE TOP COVER PIECE, 40"X 26"

B AND H—TWO LONG PIECES, 40"X 6"

E—ONE BOTTOM PIECE, 40"X 26"

I—SIX SPACERS, 6"X 1⅞"

STEPS:

① ASSEMBLE PARTS A, B, AND E WITH WHITE GLUE AND STRAIGHT PINS PUSHED IN LIKE NAILS.

② MARK SHELF PLACEMENTS 2" APART, AND GLUE THE FIRST SPACERS AT THE BACK OF E TO SUPPORT SHELF D. GLUE EDGES OF D AND FIX IN PLACE WITH PINS. REPEAT FOR SHELF C. PROP THE SHELVES' LOOSE ENDS AND LET DRY.

③ GLUE ON END PIECE F AND TOP COVER G. SECURE THEM WITH PINS AND LET DRY.

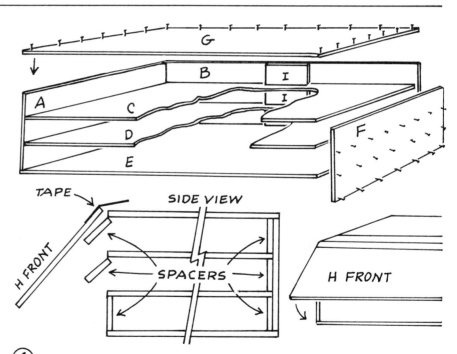

④ TAPE-HINGE FRONT SPACERS ON SHELVES AS SHOWN FOR SHELF SUPPORT.

⑤ TAPE-HINGE FRONT COVER H. IT WILL HELP KEEP DUST OFF THE STORED PAPERS.

Adhesives

White Glue such as Elmer's, Sobo, and Polyvinyl Acetate (PVA) bonds well and dries clear and shiny. It dilutes with water, which works best on heavyweight paper and card stock because the water causes lighter-weight paper to warp. Apply white glue conservatively, and spread it well. It holds glitter better than other glues. To clean up, wash hands in warm water.

Glue Sticks work well even on lightweight paper, and are especially good for sealing handmade envelopes. The tubes and dispensers make for easy storage and portability. Each tube holds about ¼ ounce of odorless glue. Either dot or smear the glue onto the paper. It washes off hands and clothes with water.

Spray Adhesive comes in an aerosol can. One quick coat on the back of a piece of art leaves you a few seconds to position it. For instant adhesion, spray both the art and mounting board. Let them dry before pressing them together. Acetone (rubber cement thinner) will get them to separate again. Apply the acetone with a cotton swab to clean up the edges. Contain the spray with a "spray barn".

Fusible Webbing is adhesive on a webbed backing that adheres to fabric to stiffen it so it can be cut into collage elements. Buy it by the yard at a fabric store. It comes in several thicknesses and is ironed onto the back of fabric such as knit material. Bonding tape is a narrow ribbon-like version that fuses trim such as lace to fabric.

Rubber Cement

is brushed on but is otherwise used like spray adhesives. Acetone thins it and cleans up smears. Rubber cement will not buckle lightweight paper, and can be applied fairly thick. It will eventually lose its tackiness and discolor the paper.

Mounting Boards

are mat boards with a peel-off covering protecting one sticky side. Craft stores sell them for mounting needlework. Use them on greeting cards to back fabric and decorative paper, or for stand-up cards and booklet covers.

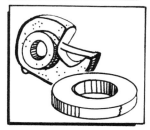

Electric Hot Guns

look like soldering irons. They melt clear stick glue and dispense it through a nozzle. The glue dries quickly but is thick and hard. It will hold together 3-dimensional elements, such as wood pieces, but will pop off flexible surfaces.

Double-Stick Tape

has adhesive on both sides, and comes in a roll. It mounts elements well, and can be a spot-anchor to keep them from shifting. It loses its tackiness in time, and sometimes discolors the paper.

Clear Contact® Paper

brand adhesive plastic is an old standby. It comes in 18" wide rolls, and has a peel-off backing. Use it to cover dried flowers or other collage elements. Also use it to cover an address lettered on an envelope in water-soluble ink. Acetone will dissolve the adhesive if the Contact® Paper needs to be removed. Run a few drops under the edge and lift.

Mucilage glue is a holdover from the past. It is made from animal and vegetable sources, and is inexpensive. It turns brittle in time.

liquid Adhesive comes in roll-on bottles and buckles lightweight paper. It is an all-purpose glue that cleans up with water.

Removable Tape (also drafting tape) comes in dispensers or rolls, like cellophane tape. Use it to hold down overlays or to attach a guide sheet to the back of paper. Removable tape peels off readily without damaging the paper underneath.

Spray Barn

Cut one side out of a brown paper grocery sack to contain aerosol spray adhesives.

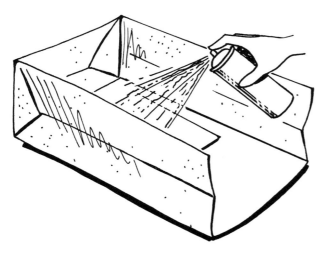

Waste Paper

Use old catalogs or magazines under paste-up elements to protect the table when putting on the glue. Rip off each used sheet to expose a clean one.

Paper Grain

The process by which paper is made causes the fibers to line up in one direction. This is called the grain. A fold that is made across the grain will be stiff and broken. A fold made with the grain will be flexible and smooth. It is important to know the direction of the grain when making greeting cards because of the folding involved. The following methods will help you find the grain in a piece of paper, using a test piece.

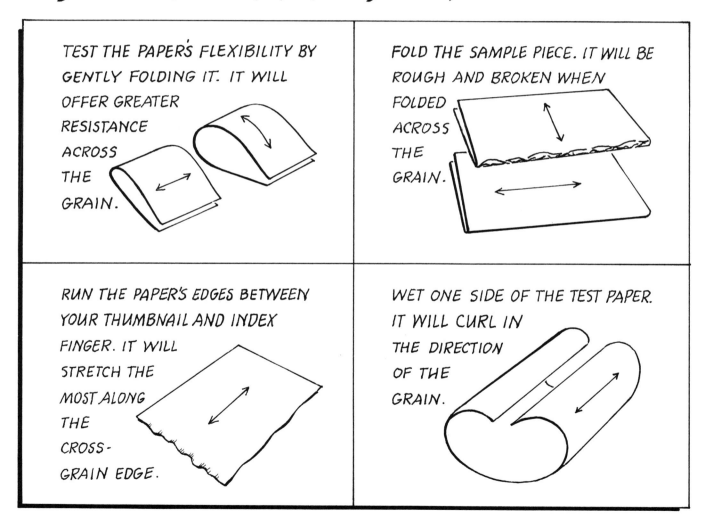

TEST THE PAPER'S FLEXIBILITY BY GENTLY FOLDING IT. IT WILL OFFER GREATER RESISTANCE ACROSS THE GRAIN.

FOLD THE SAMPLE PIECE. IT WILL BE ROUGH AND BROKEN WHEN FOLDED ACROSS THE GRAIN.

RUN THE PAPER'S EDGES BETWEEN YOUR THUMBNAIL AND INDEX FINGER. IT WILL STRETCH THE MOST ALONG THE CROSS-GRAIN EDGE.

WET ONE SIDE OF THE TEST PAPER. IT WILL CURL IN THE DIRECTION OF THE GRAIN.

Cutting Tips

To get the best results from a paper cutter, lay a ruler on top of the paper, close against the edge. Hold it down during cutting. This makes sure the paper does not accidentally shift, leaving a curved edge.

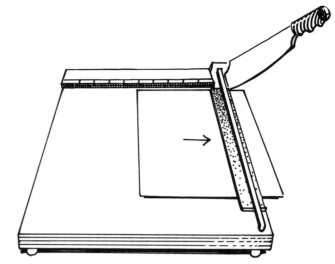

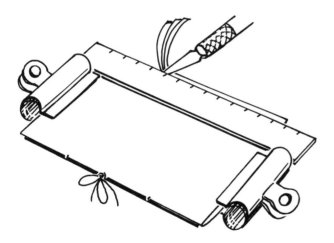

Cards made in booket form sometimes need their edges trimmed and squared. Keep the pages from shifting by clamping them tightly between bulldog clips. Also, cut against a steel-edged ruler.

Make perforated lines in cards where you want to tear apart two sections. Do this by running a pounce wheel along a ruler. Protect the table with a piece of cardboard.

Card Folds

Fold the card in the direction of the paper's grain to get a smooth crease. If you fold it against the grain the crease will be rough and broken. Test a scrap to find its grain direction. Then plan the folds to run with the grain.

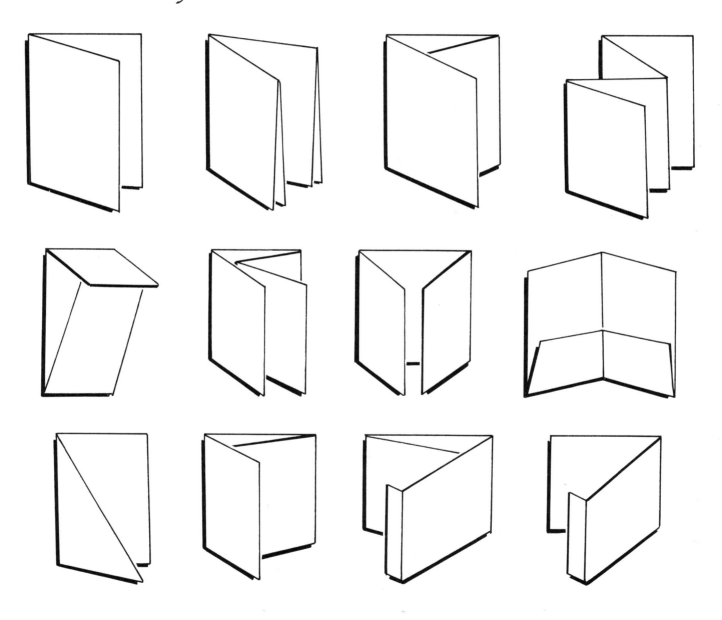

Deckle and Other Edges

Handmade paper is made in a mold. The detachable wooden frame around the outside edges of the mold is called a deckle. When the deckle is removed, it leaves behind a rough, untrimmed edge. You can deckle any paper using the following techniques. Deckle your card before lettering it so that if you ruin the paper, that is all you have ruined.

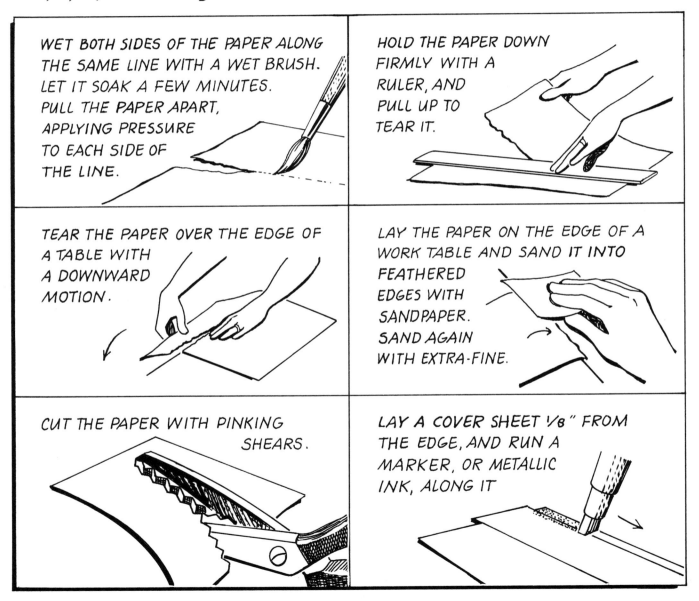

WET BOTH SIDES OF THE PAPER ALONG THE SAME LINE WITH A WET BRUSH. LET IT SOAK A FEW MINUTES. PULL THE PAPER APART, APPLYING PRESSURE TO EACH SIDE OF THE LINE.

HOLD THE PAPER DOWN FIRMLY WITH A RULER, AND PULL UP TO TEAR IT.

TEAR THE PAPER OVER THE EDGE OF A TABLE WITH A DOWNWARD MOTION.

LAY THE PAPER ON THE EDGE OF A WORK TABLE AND SAND IT INTO FEATHERED EDGES WITH SANDPAPER. SAND AGAIN WITH EXTRA-FINE.

CUT THE PAPER WITH PINKING SHEARS.

LAY A COVER SHEET 1/8" FROM THE EDGE, AND RUN A MARKER, OR METALLIC INK, ALONG IT

Drying Rack for Greeting Cards HOLDS TEN

From a 14"x 17" sheet of bristol board, cut four strips, each measuring 3½" X 17". Glue or tape them end to end by overlapping them ¼"so that you end up with one long strip 50½" long. Measure ¾"at one end and ⅜"at the other. Turn these up to later staple to a base. Cut the base from matboard to measure 3½" X 12".

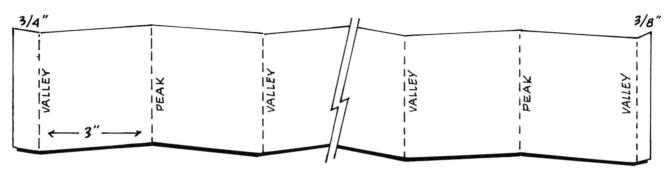

Measure and score lines on the long strip every 3", then fold accordion-style. Staple the ends to the base. Slip large rubber bands over every other valley fold. Pull the folds to the near end and stack the damp cards from back to front. Once they are dry, push the cards together to open up the near-end folds.

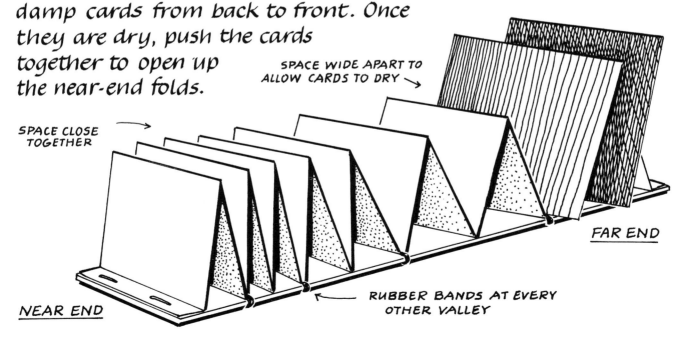

21

LETTERING

Once you have prepared your work area and your card stock, and have selected the wording for your card's message, you must decide which style of lettering or alphabet to use. Every alphabet – whether hand-rendered or typeset – conveys its own tone. The five calligraphic alphabets that follow are popular, but there are many more. <u>Tips on Type</u>, <u>Lettering Tips</u>, and <u>Calligraphy Tips</u>, all by Bill Gray, have more alphabets from which to choose as well as other information to help artists perfect their lettering technique.

Black Letter

THIS ALPHABET IS MADE WITH A CALLIGRAPHY PEN. NOTICE THAT THE SMALL LETTERS INTERSECT THE WAIST AND BASE LINES, BUT FALL INSIDE THE ASCENDING AND DESCENDING LINES. THE CAPITALS INTERSECT THE BASE LINE ONLY. USE A 45° PEN ANGLE, AND SPACE THE LETTERS CLOSE WITHIN WORDS.

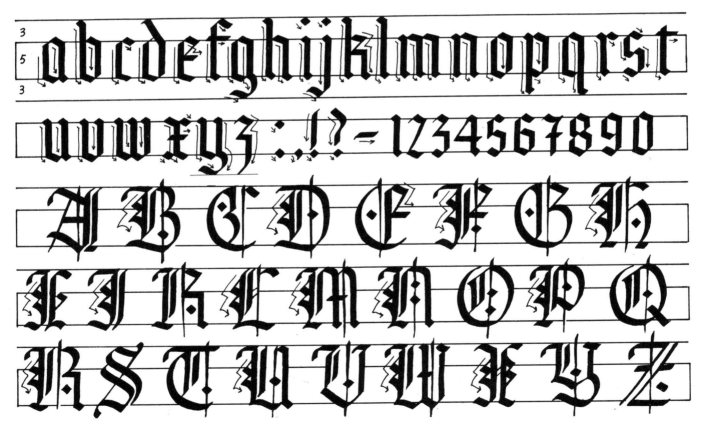

Chancery Cursive (Cursive Italic)

The calligraphic alphabet shown below requires a chisel pen. Speedball makes dip pens; Platignum fountain pens, and Sanford colored markers. There are other brands, too. Hold the square tip of the nib at a 45° angle to the base line so the widths of the horizontal and vertical strokes in the letters are the same. Slant the letters as in handwriting. Use the arrows to help with stroke direction and sequence. Use guide lines that are five pen widths apart for ascenders, bodies, and descenders. Capitals are two pen widths shorter than ascenders.

Stick Alphabet

Here is a simple all-capital alphabet that is easy to make. It has a happy look that works perfectly for greeting cards and addresses on envelopes. Make the stick letters first. Then add dots to the ends of lines. Letter against a ruler to keep the lines straight. Use colored felt-tip pens, metallic, or opaque pens (which show up well on dark paper). Get variety by lettering each word or line in a different color. These letters look good with rubber stamp illustrations.

Script

Use a "copperplate" or "script" pen which has a pointed, flexible nib. The thick strokes are made by pressing hard on down-strokes; the thin ones by pressing only lightly on up-strokes. Be sure the nib is lined up with the stroke as shown in the left illustration. Right-handers need to use either an elbow

pen, or turn their paper in such a way as to get the correct slant on the letters.

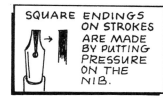

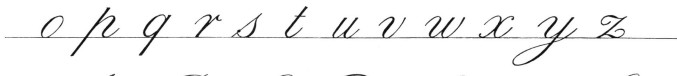

a b c d e f g h i j k l m n

o p q r s t u v w x y z

A B C D E F G

H I J K L M N O

P 2 R S T U V

12345   V W X Y Z   67890

Neuland

THIS BOLD ALPHABET WORKS WELL ON GREETING CARDS. SEE LAYOUT OPTIONS ON THE FACING PAGE. USE ANY WIDTH CALLIGRAPHY PEN AND MEASURE THE HEIGHT AT 4 PEN WIDTHS (WIDE PENS MAKE LARGE LETTERS AND NARROW PENS MAKE SMALL LETTERS). HOLD THE PEN AT EITHER A HORIZONTAL OR VERTICAL ANGLE, DEPENDING ON THE STROKE, AND FOLLOW THE ARROWS FOR THE STROKE DIRECTION.

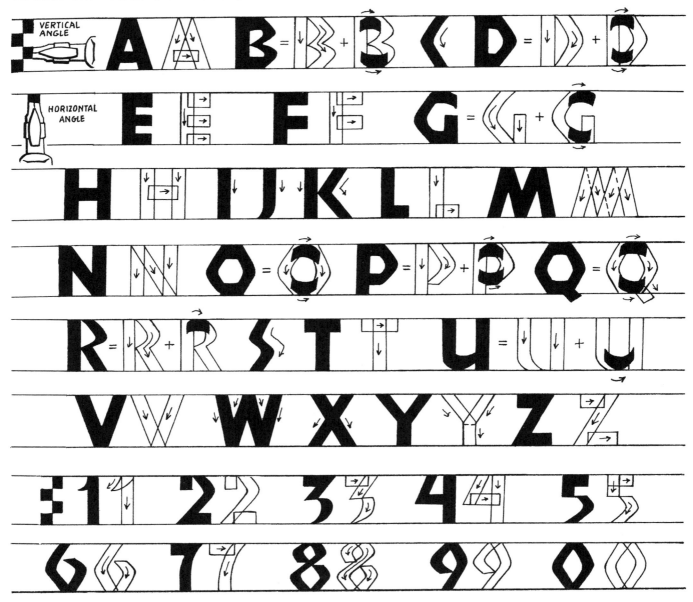

Ways To Use Neuland

Draw curved lines with a template, leaving no space between the lines.

Draw bars between the lines of lettering. The quote can be cut out with a mat knife and mounted on colored paper.

Letter a short phrase and repeat it to make a pattern. Do not put a space between words or lines. Use straight margins on both sides.

After lettering a phrase, put it on a lightbox and ink in only the negative shapes.

Decorated Letters

The system for decorating letters for a historic look is quite simple. Choose one of the letters shown below, and enlarge it with a photocopier. Trace it onto a greeting card. Make the letter itself black or red. Then decorate it in another color with a fine-point marker.

1. Outline the letter with a box. Then "inline" the negative shapes.

2. Draw "cusps" in the triangles to make them look like leaves.

3. Draw "button ferns" in the long rectangular spaces. These look like stems with rounded leaves.

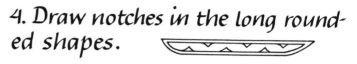

4. Draw notches in the long rounded shapes.

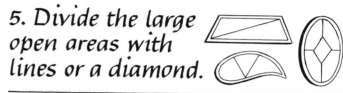

5. Divide the large open areas with lines or a diamond.

6. Inline the new shapes.

7. Put button ferns, cusps, or "golf clubs" in the new spaces.

8. Add curls at the corners and in the middle of the large box. Space "footlights" between them.

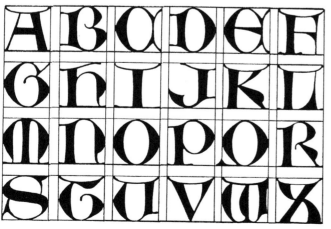

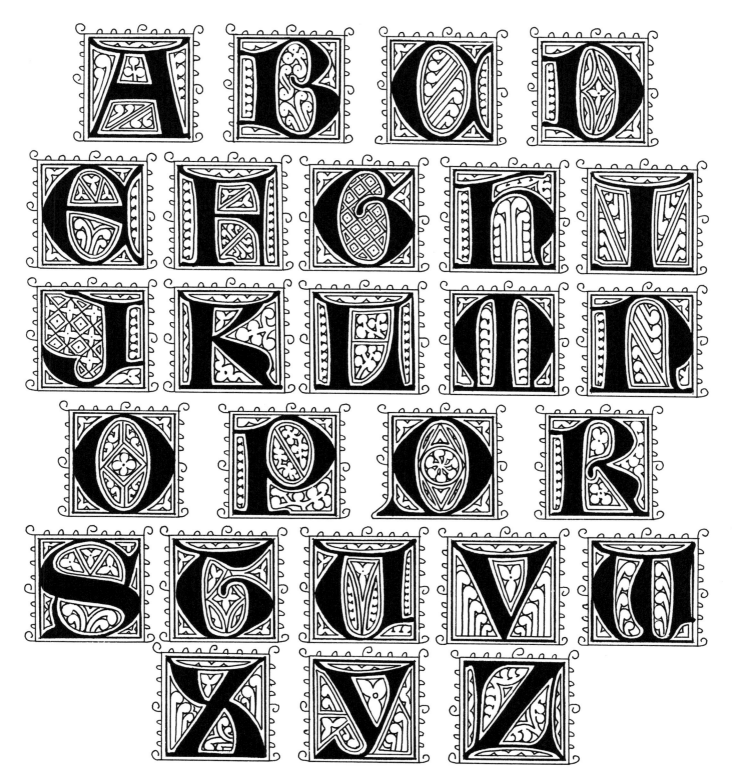

Transfer Letters

Dry transfer letters that are burnished onto cards come in several brands: Letraset, Formatt, Zipatone, DECA^dry, Chartpak, and others. Some have letters printed on adhesive film that is cut apart for burnishing down. Others print the letters on the film in reverse so each letter is burnished down individually, after which the film is removed. To keep these letters from cracking burnish on a hard surface. Also, burnish only the letter and not the surrounding area.

GIORGIO
Style number 530

ABCDEFGHIJKLMNOP
QRSTUVWXYZÆŒØ1
234567890(&$!?£¢%/*)
«»::~∨∧‥∘∘·,,‥∘

530-72CN 72pt. 19mm   530-60CN 60pt. 15.9mm

530-48CN 48pt. 12.5mm   530-36CN 36pt. 9.5mm   530-24CN 24pt. 6.2mm   530-18CN 18pt. 4.5mm

ABOVE: ZIPATONE LETTERS IN SIX SIZES.

Practice using transfer letters so you can line them up and space them properly. Spray Letraset brand with fixative to make them more durable.

RIGHT: FIVE OF THE STYLES MADE BY FORMATT. ▶

AMERICAN TEXT

ABCDEFGHIJKLMNOPQRST
UVWXYZ&abcdefghijklmnopqrst
uvwxyz$¢1234567890.,:;-!?'""[ ]

AMERICAN TYPEWRITER BOLD

ABCDEFGHIJKLMNOP
QRSTUVWXYZ&abcdef
ghijklmnopqrstuvwxy
z$¢1234567890.,:;-!?()%

AMERICAN UNCIAL

ABCDEFGHIJKLMNOPQRST
UVWXYZ&abcdefghijklmn
opqrstuvwxyz$1 234567
890.,-:;!?'ABCDEFGHIJK
LMNOPQRSTUVWXYZ

ANGLO

ABCDEFGHIJKLMNOPQR
STUVWXYZ&abcdefghijkl
mnopqrstuvwxyz$¢1234
567890.,:;-!?'""()%

ANTIQUE BOLD

ABCDEFGHIJKLMNO
PQRSTUVWXYZ&abcd
efghijklmnopqrstuvwx
yz$1234567890.,-:;!?'"()

Transfer Graphics

The companies that make transfer letters also make transfer graphics. These are usually sold in black and white, but border tapes are available in colors. Form-X-Film self-adhesive vinyl film comes in colors. It sells in both transparent and opaque versions. Look for these in stores that sell graphic-art supplies.

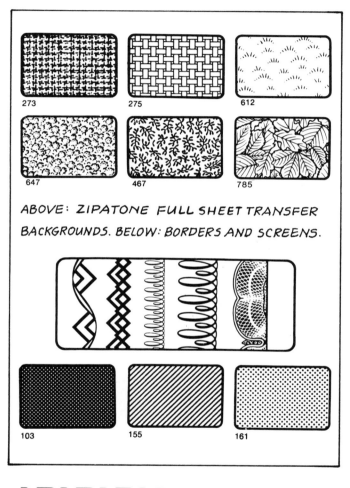

273 275 612
647 467 785

ABOVE: ZIPATONE FULL SHEET TRANSFER BACKGROUNDS. BELOW: BORDERS AND SCREENS.

103 155 161

THE BORDERS AND GRAPHICS HERE ARE BY FORMATT.

6437

No. 6422

6645

6644

No. 6880

7370K
7368K
7371K
7373K
7372K

FORMALINE BORDER TAPES COME IN ROLLS LIKE CELLOPHANE TAPE AND BURNISH DOWN.

Stencils and Templates

Stencils and templates come in many sizes, and will help you with both the lettering and illustration on cards.

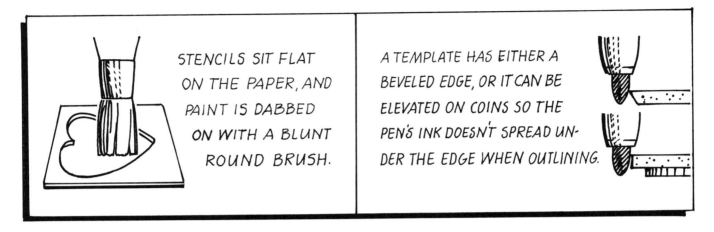

STENCILS SIT FLAT ON THE PAPER, AND PAINT IS DABBED ON WITH A BLUNT ROUND BRUSH.

A TEMPLATE HAS EITHER A BEVELED EDGE, OR IT CAN BE ELEVATED ON COINS SO THE PEN'S INK DOESN'T SPREAD UNDER THE EDGE WHEN OUTLINING.

Paint in outlined shapes or cut shapes out of decorative paper for collage elements. Use templates to cut windows in cards to back with clear acetate. Make your own stencils and templates from heavy acetate or oaktag paper.

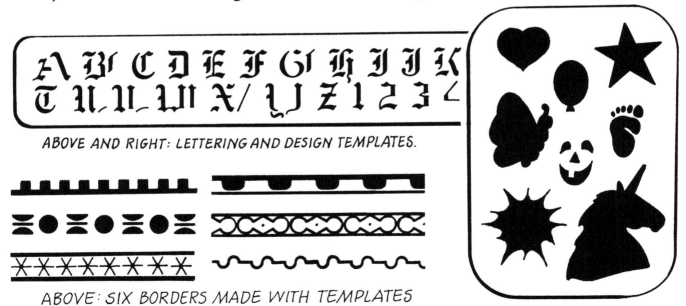

ABOVE AND RIGHT: LETTERING AND DESIGN TEMPLATES.

ABOVE: SIX BORDERS MADE WITH TEMPLATES

Borders

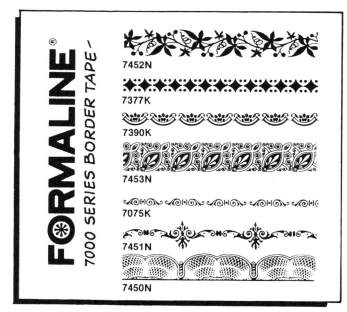

There are different options for making borders on greeting cards. Stores that sell graphic-art supplies have border tape that comes in rolls, some in color. Graphic Products Corporation publishes Graphic Source Clip Art books that contain copyright-free camera-ready art printed on one side of reproduction-quality dull enamel paper.

Borders are made up of one small design repeated many times. When making your own, design a corner, too. You can flip the design (reverse it) for variety.

  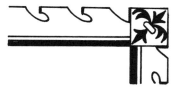

USE WRAPPING PAPER FOR A BORDER ON THE CARD SO IT MATCHES THE GIFT:

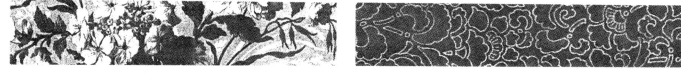

OUTLINE THE BORDER IN BLACK. COLOR IT, OR FILL IT IN AS SHOWN HERE:

WASH   STIPPLE   CROSSHATCH   DIAPER PATTERN   WATER SPOT

PRINTING TECHNIQUES

Printing techniques offer nice graphic effects and make it easy to make multiple greeting cards. The simplest technique is stamping.

Rubber Stamps

SUPPLIES:

* STAEDTLER-MARS OR FACTIS PLASTIC ERASERS
* ACETONE OR NAIL POLISH REMOVER AND COTTON BALLS
* TRACING PAPER
* POINTED MAT KNIFE
* SPEEDBALL LINOLEUM CUTTING SET
* SOFT PENCIL (B OR HB)
* OPTIONAL: SEWING NEEDLE, CORK OR DOWEL

Draw your design on tracing paper in pencil, darkening the image instead of outlining it. Clean the eraser with acetone, and lay the drawing on it, pencil side down. Burnish the design with your thumbnail to transfer the image. Remove the paper and use a pencil to touch up the image, which will be reversed, but will print right side up.

To transfer a printed design, photocopy it. Lay the copy face down on the eraser and sponge the back with an acetone-soaked cotton ball, pressing firmly. The image will transfer.

For calligraphy, letter it in water-soluble ink. Wet the eraser and blot it nearly dry. Lay the calligraphy face down on the eraser and dampen the back with water to transfer the lettering.

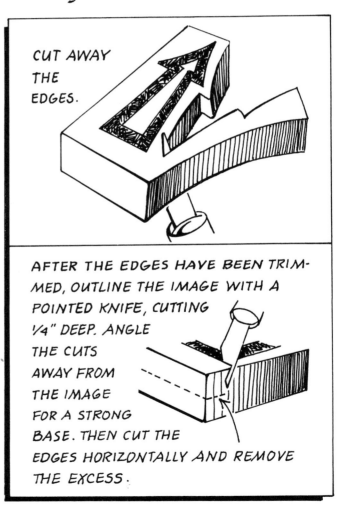

CUT AWAY THE EDGES.

AFTER THE EDGES HAVE BEEN TRIMMED, OUTLINE THE IMAGE WITH A POINTED KNIFE, CUTTING 1/4" DEEP. ANGLE THE CUTS AWAY FROM THE IMAGE FOR A STRONG BASE. THEN CUT THE EDGES HORIZONTALLY AND REMOVE THE EXCESS.

Use the scrap you cut away to make small stamps mounted on push pins. While cutting the stamp, set it on a bottle cap turned upside down or on a small piece of tracing paper. This helps you turn the eraser to get the best cutting angle. Hold the knife still and move the eraser to avoid making a sudden uncontrolled cut.

Use the V-shaped scoop knife to outline the various shapes. Then use a larger scoop to remove the middle.

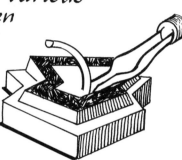

Linoleum cutters and mat knives are too unwieldy for cutting fine detail. Use instead a needle sharpened on Arkansas whetstone and mounted in a cork or dowel. Run the needle around a template to create curves and circles. Punch small dots with the tip of a re- tracted ballpoint pen and remove the centers.

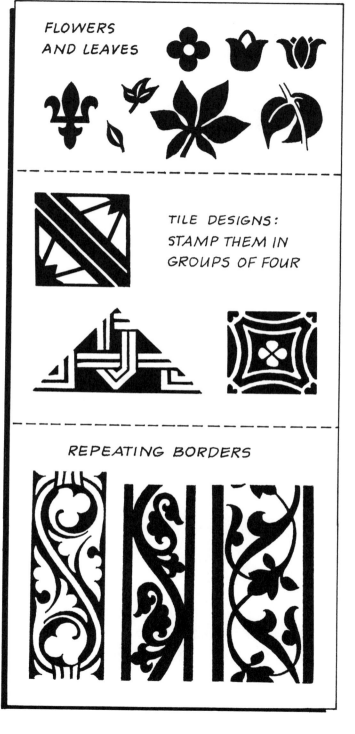

FLOWERS AND LEAVES

TILE DESIGNS: STAMP THEM IN GROUPS OF FOUR

REPEATING BORDERS

Color in Rubber Stamps

Color is part of the fun of stamping. Standard stamp pads come in three kinds: felt, foam, and micropore. The felt pads ink the stamp evenly but dry out the quickest. Foam ones are too soft and get ink on the background. Micropore are the most expensive, and have a limited number of colors. You can also buy rainbow pads with three colors in bands or dry pads in which you put watercolor. Try coloring the stamp by hand with felt pens for interesting variations.

IDEAS:

Make a large design by cutting it out of several erasers. Tape them together around their edges first and draw a grid in felt-tip pen on the back. Use the grid to align the pieces when setting them down one at a time for stamping. Or keep them taped together if they are not unwieldy.

You can make stationery sets by decorating writing paper, envelopes, and wrapping paper with the same stamp or stamps. Use stamps to add repeat patterns on a layout. Flip a design by photocopying it onto tracing paper and drawing it again on the back side before transferring it to an eraser.

Different Kinds of Stamps

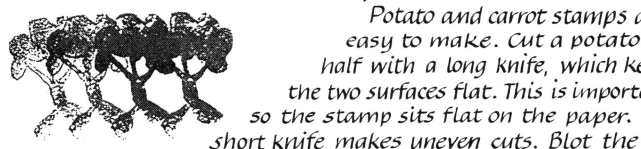

PRINT A POTATO STAMP SEVERAL TIMES FOR A FOREST

Potato and carrot stamps are easy to make. Cut a potato in half with a long knife, which keeps the two surfaces flat. This is important so the stamp sits flat on the paper. A short knife makes uneven cuts. Blot the potato dry and draw on it with a marker. Remove the background with a pointed mat knife. Angle the cuts away to give the image a strong base. Or press a cookie cutter into the potato and cut off the excess potato before removing the cutter. To make a stamp pad, put a square of felt in a saucer and saturate it with ink. Use carrots to make smaller stamps. Slice an apple and print it in red ink. Add seeds and a black stem. Even fingerprints make interesting stamps.

CARROT MOON

FIST AND FINGERTIPS

FINGERPRINTS

Embossing

Embossing is raising an image in relief. You can emboss by making a template and pressing paper into it. The template is good for many copies and can be kept for future projects. Embossing looks good on monograms, borders, and decorated letters.

SUPPLIES: POINTED MAT KNIFE; GRAPHITE STICK; WHITE PAPER WITHOUT A STIFF GRAIN (TRY STRATHMORE 1-PLY BRISTOL); TRACING PAPER; TAPE; 3 BURNISHERS (A ROUNDED SPOON, A BONE FOLDER OR LARGE KNITTING NEEDLE, AND A COMMERCIAL BALLPOINT BURNISHER OR SIMILARLY POINTED IMPLEMENT); CLEAR ACETATE SHEETS 0.01 (10 mil) THICKNESS (0.0075 ALSO WORKS) OR 4-PLY BRISTOL BOARD FOR THE TEMPLATE; LIGHT BOX (IF YOU USE A BRISTOL BOARD TEMPLATE); COLD-PRESS ILLUSTRATION BOARD FOR BACKING THE TEMPLATE; ADHESIVE SUCH AS GLUE STICK, RUBBER CEMENT, OR SPRAY ADHESIVE FOR MOUNTING THE TEMPLATE.

CUTTING THE TEMPLATE

Lay the clear acetate on the artwork and cut around the image with the mat knife. Overcut the corners so they meet. Pull the knife in down-strokes, turning the art. If the knife slips, repair the cut with tape. Bend the acetate and pop out the pieces to be sure they are free. Then re-place them.

THE ACETATE IS LAID OVER THE ART. USE A LIGHT BOX FOR A BRISTOL TEMPLATE.

MOUNTING THE TEMPLATE

Mount the acetate or bristol template securely to the illustration board with glue stick, rubber cement, or spray adhesive. Do this by applying the adhesive to the front of the template as it lays on the table, and pressing the illustration board down on it lightly. Be sure all the pieces are in place. Turn the template over and remove the positive shapes. Then burnish down the negative shapes.

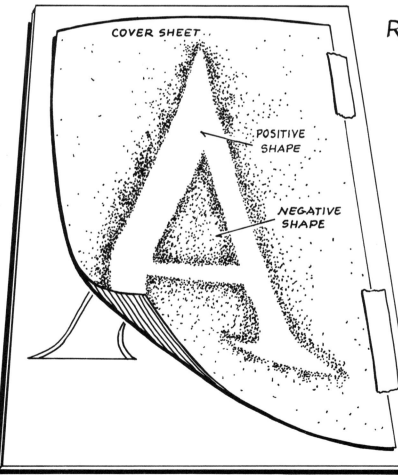

COVER SHEET

POSITIVE SHAPE

NEGATIVE SHAPE

REGISTERING THE ART

Cover the template with a sheet of tracing paper and tape it down along one edge. Use a graphite stick to rub an outline of the image. Spray it with fixative to keep it from smudging. Slip your good paper under this sheet and position the art on it. Tape it down and fold the tracing paper out of the way to emboss.

EMBOSSING THE ART – DRY METHOD

Rub the bowl of a spoon over the back of the paper to begin stretching it. Working this way helps insure that the paper will not tear later.

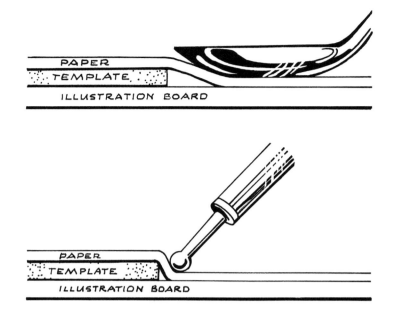

Next, change to the large knitting needle to define the edges. Increase the pressure with each pass. Then use the ballpoint burnisher to make the edges crisp.

WET METHOD

The wet method of embossing works well only on the acetate template. Bristol templates absorb the water, which softens their edges. Some artists soak the entire sheet of paper to emboss it, but this can ruin the size. It's also difficult to keep it clean as you work. Instead, use a cotton swab to wet down only the line to be embossed. Then use plastic or wooden tools instead of metal. This method gets extra stretch out of the paper for more detail. A paper that works well is 140-pound hot-press watercolor. If you find yourself tearing the paper, place a cover sheet on top of the wetted paper before embossing.

Block Printing

Linoleum blocks are easier to cut than wood ones because they have a softer texture and no grain. The linoleum comes glued to pressed wood blocks. When the gray or tan surface is cut away it exposes another color. The contrast marks the edges and shapes clearly. Use the following supplies to make block print illustrations for your greeting cards:

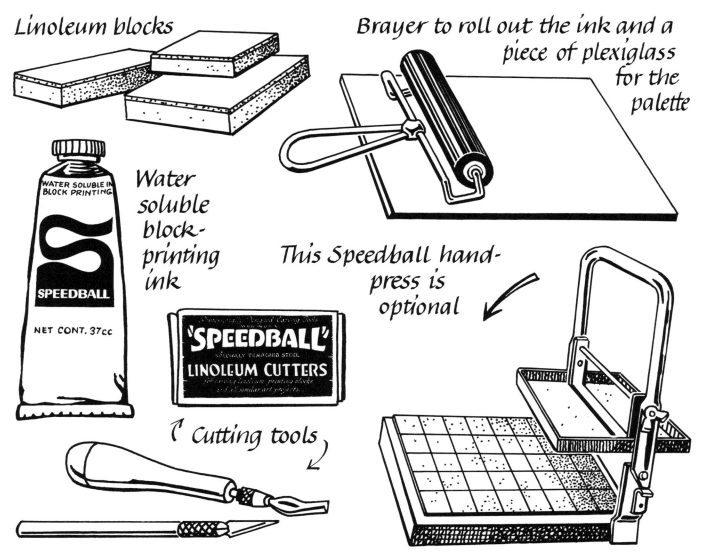

Linoleum blocks

Brayer to roll out the ink and a piece of plexiglass for the palette

WATER SOLUBLE IN BLOCK PRINTING

S

SPEEDBALL

NET CONT. 37cc

Water soluble block-printing ink

"SPEEDBALL"

SPECIALLY TEMPERED STEEL

LINOLEUM CUTTERS

This Speedball hand-press is optional

Cutting tools

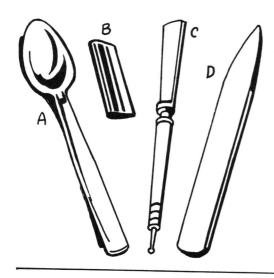

If you don't use the hand press, use one of these tools to burnish the paper down onto the inked block.

A. Tablespoon

B. Small rubber squeegie

C. Commercial double-ended burnisher

D. Bone or plastic folder

TRACING THE DESIGN

THE IMAGE ON THE BLOCK PRINTS IN REVERSE, SO THE MIRROR-IMAGE OF THE DESIGN HAS TO BE TRACED ONTO THE BLOCK TO GET THE DESIGN TO PRINT CORRECTLY.

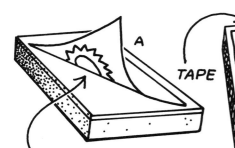

PENCIL SIDE DOWN

TAPE

Tape a pencil drawing face down (A) on the block and burnish it (B) to transfer the design. Do the original in an HB or softer pencil for the best results.

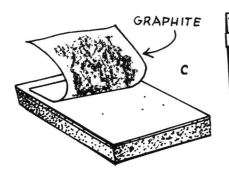

GRAPHITE

Or rub graphite on the back of the art (C). Tape it to the block, graphite side down, and trace over the design (D) with a ballpoint pen or hard pencil. Touch up the design afterwards. (Make sure the original design accounts for the image reversal mentioned above.)

Cutting Linoleum Blocks

ANGLE THE CUTS AWAY FROM THE IMAGE

MAKE V-SHAPED CUTS AROUND THE IMAGE

First, darken the positive shapes so you know at a glance which area to cut away. Then take a pointed knife and cut around the image at a slant to give it a strong base. Use a ruler or template where needed. Rotate the block often to get a comfortable angle with the knife. Make V-shaped cuts to separate the image from its background before scooping out the background.

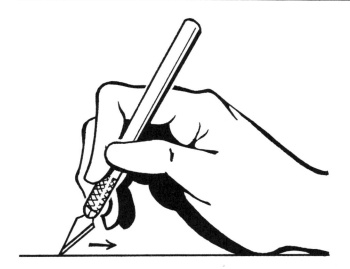

Anchor the heel of your hand to keep the cutting motion in your fingers. This prevents the knife from slipping accidentally. Use steady, even pressure.

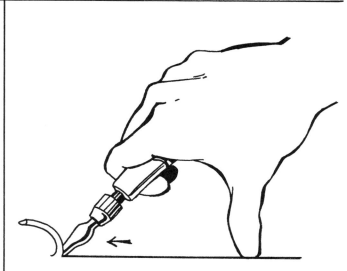

Scoop out large areas. Again, anchor your hand so the movement is in your fingers. Print the design once or twice as you work to test your progress.

Inking and Printing

Squeeze a line of ink across the palette and roll it out with the brayer. Use the brayer to ink the block. Try to hit all the high surfaces without filling in the low areas. If the block gets too much ink on it, make two prints from it before inking again. If some of the background picks up ink, cut it out with a knife.

INKING THE PALETTE   INKING THE BLOCK

Put drafting tape on the edges of the paper before laying it on the block. Secure the paper to the block and smooth down the paper with your fingers. Burnish the entire design while being careful not to move the paper. Remove the paper and let it air-dry.

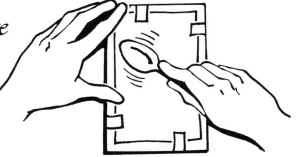

Here are some ideas: Ink up a leaf or other object and print it on the linoleum. Then cut it into a block print. For variety, use white glue on the block instead of ink. Print the glue image and sprinkle with glitter.

You're Invited To Thanksgiving At Our House

I LOVE YOU

An Easter Prayer

Silk-Screen Printing

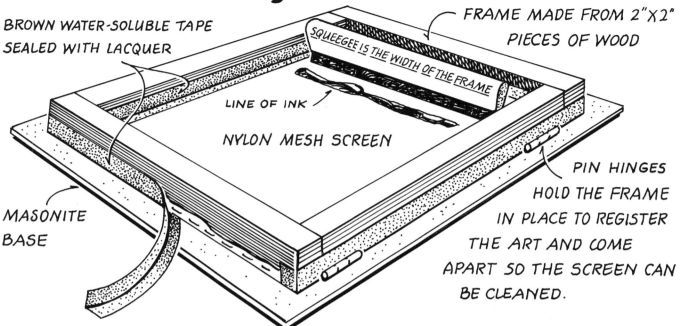

BROWN WATER-SOLUBLE TAPE SEALED WITH LACQUER

FRAME MADE FROM 2"×2" PIECES OF WOOD

SQUEEGEE IS THE WIDTH OF THE FRAME

LINE OF INK

NYLON MESH SCREEN

PIN HINGES HOLD THE FRAME IN PLACE TO REGISTER THE ART AND COME APART SO THE SCREEN CAN BE CLEANED.

MASONITE BASE

THE NYLON MESH SCREEN IS STRETCHED AND STAPLED OVER THE EDGE OF THE FRAME, THEN COVERED WITH WATER-SOLUBLE PAPER TAPE.

The versatility of a silk-screen will help you mass-produce greeting cards of consistent quality in many colors. The above diagram shows a homemade silk-screen setup. It can be made to any dimensions and reused many times. The squeegee distributes ink across the nylon mesh through the stencil design on it. The ink prints on paper registered under the screen on the masonite base. Use tape as shown here to help position the paper. Prepare a new screen by scrubbing it with soap and water (use a hand brush). Clean ink and paint out of the screen with the appropriate solvent.

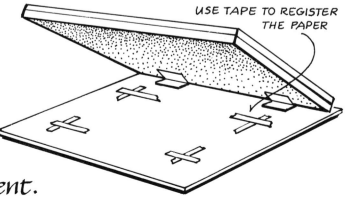

USE TAPE TO REGISTER THE PAPER

Silk-Screen Stencils

PAPER STENCIL

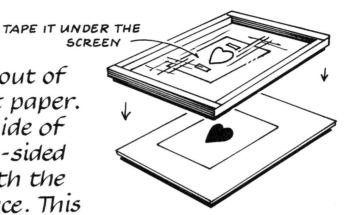

TAPE IT UNDER THE SCREEN

Cut the negative shape out of medium to lightweight paper. Attach it to the underside of the screen with double-sided tape. The first pass with the squeegee holds it in place. This works for simple shapes and adding background color, but paper stencils do not hold up very long.

LACQUER STENCIL

SWAB THE TOP SIDE

Paint a film of green lacquer onto an acetate or Mylar sheet. When it is dry, use a sharp knife to outline the design, cutting through only the lacquer; then remove the positive shapes (the areas you want to print) by peeling them off. Lay the acetate under the screen and swab it from the top side with lacquer thinner to make the design transfer onto the screen. The acetate should peel away.

GLUE STENCIL

Cover the original drawing with acetate and put it under the screen. Trace it with a brush and glue that is water-soluble when dry. Use LePage's Original or diluted white glue to paint in the negative shapes on the screen.

THE ACETATE PROTECTS THE ART FROM THE GLUE

ACETATE

ARTWORK

PHOTOGRAPHIC STENCIL

For this use Photo Emulsion and Sensitizer (sold at art-supply stores). Mix together 4 parts Photo Emulsion to 1 part Sensitizer, then spread an even, thin layer on the screen. Dry the coated screen in the dark for about an hour. Prepare the art by drawing it in India ink on tracing paper. Or draw on wet-media acetate. Arrange the screen and art as shown to the right. Use a 150-watt bulb with a reflector pan. Hang it over the screen 12" away, centered. Expose screens measuring up to 12"x18" 45 minutes to 1½ hours.

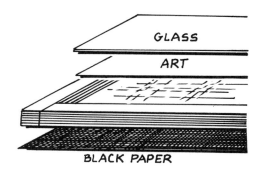

GLASS

ART

BLACK PAPER

TO TRANSFER THE ART, LAY THE SCREEN ON BLACK PAPER. DRAW THE DESIGN ON TRANSLUCENT PAPER AND LAY IT RIGHT SIDE UP ON THE SCREEN. KEEP IT FLAT DURING ITS EXPOSURE TO LIGHT BY COVERING IT WITH A PIECE OF GLASS.

After the screen has been exposed to the light, rinse away the unexposed emulsion under the ink lines by spraying it forcefully with water. Dry the screen before printing it.

PRINTING A SILK SCREEN

Test-print the design to be sure the stencil has no flaws and to register the paper correctly. Keep hands and tools clean with paper towels. ① Pour a line of ink along the far edge of the screen. ② Hold the frame down with one hand and pull the ink across the design with the squeegee. ③ Return the leftover ink to the far end. Lift the screen and replace the paper to make the next print. Clean the screen before storing it.

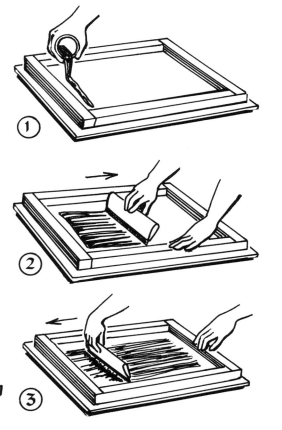

Acrylic Marbling

Acrylic marbling will stick to paper, leather, cloth, and wood. Use it on envelopes and liners, wrapping paper, booklet covers, and collage elements. Color examples of marbling are on pages 70 and 71. The instructions here are for a professional approach to marbling. The illustration shows the equipment you will need and how to arrange it. You will also need a sink. Do not use water that has sulfur or calcium in it to mix the ingredients. Use distilled water instead. Mix the ingredients the day before so they age and come to room temperature.

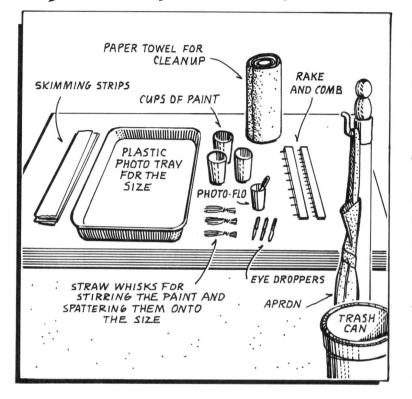

PAPER TOWEL FOR CLEANUP

SKIMMING STRIPS

CUPS OF PAINT

RAKE AND COMB

PLASTIC PHOTO TRAY FOR THE SIZE

PHOTO-FLO

STRAW WHISKS FOR STIRRING THE PAINT AND SPATTERING THEM ONTO THE SIZE

EYE DROPPERS

APRON

TRASH CAN

SUPPLIES :

* POWDERED METHYL CELLULOSE WALLPAPER PASTE TO MAKE THE LIQUID SIZE ON WHICH THE COLORS FLOAT.

* 2" TO 3" WIDE STRIPS OF NEWSPAPER FOR SKIMMING THE USED COLORS AND SKIN OFF THE SURFACE OF THE SIZE.

* THREE COLORS OF ACRYLIC PAINT WITH AN EYE DROPPER FOR EACH COLOR.

* A SMALL BOTTLE OF PHOTO-FLO™ FOR A WETTING SOLUTION (FROM A PHOTO-SUPPLY STORE).

* SMALL JAR OF "ACRYLIC GLOSS MEDIUM & VARNISH" (FROM AN ART-MATERIALS STORE).

* MEASURING CUPS AND SPOONS, PAPER CUPS, MIXING STICKS, STACK OF NEWSPAPERS ON WHICH TO DRY THE PRINTED SHEETS.

* HOMEMADE RAKES, COMBS, AND STRAW WHISKS (SEE NEXT PAGE FOR IDEAS).

MIX THE SIZE: For each gallon of water add four or five tablespoons of methyl cellulose and two teaspoons of non-sudsing ammonia. The size can be thinned with distilled water later if it proves too thick. Leave the size overnight to age.

MIX THE PAINT: Mix two parts acrylic paint with one part water and one part Gloss Medium & Varnish.

MIX THE WETTING SOLUTION: Mix the Photo-Flo™ according to the instructions on the bottle.

BEGIN: Assemble the premixed ingredients and other supplies as shown on the previous page. Pour the size into the tray about 2" deep. Start by skimming the size with the newspaper strips. Hold each end of the skimmer; start at the far end and drag it across the surface. Then discard it. Do this after every print is made to remove leftover paint.

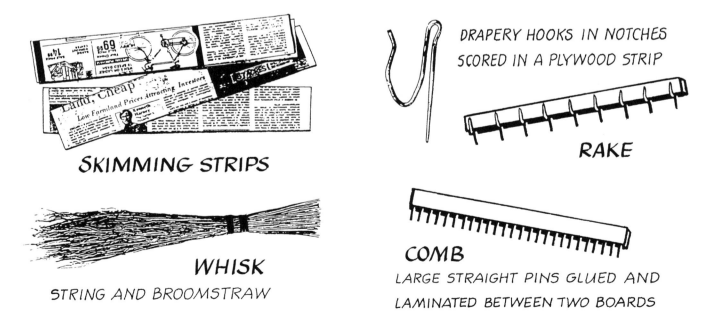

SKIMMING STRIPS

DRAPERY HOOKS IN NOTCHES
SCORED IN A PLYWOOD STRIP

RAKE

WHISK
STRING AND BROOMSTRAW

COMB
LARGE STRAIGHT PINS GLUED AND
LAMINATED BETWEEN TWO BOARDS

TESTING AND PRINTING

Test the spreadability of each color separately before making a pattern. Place one drop on the size with an eyedropper. It should spread about three inches in diameter. If the paint sinks to the bottom, thin it with room-temperature distilled water, or add a drop of Photo-Flo™. If the paint spreads too widely, add more paint to the mixture. Skim off each color before testing the next one.

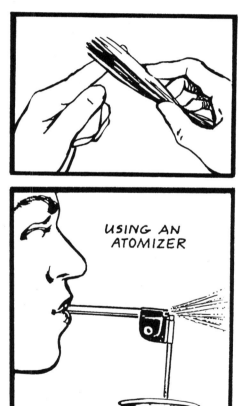

USING AN ATOMIZER

Make a pattern by first skimming the size thoroughly. Drop the colors on with an eyedropper. Or apply them by splattering them with a whisk (rap the color-filled whisk over an index finger as shown). Another method is to apply color with an atomizer. Use broom straws or homemade rakes and combs to swirl the colors into patterns.

Print the design by holding the paper at opposing corners and rolling it across the surface. This minimizes trapped air bubbles that leave holes in the pattern.

If you plop the paper onto the size, the trapped air bubbles will leave holes in the pattern. If you want blank areas for lettering a quote, lay a paper shield on the size first to block out part of the design. The shield should be wet on both sides so it won't curl. Print the design on good paper. Remove the print by one corner, rinse it and lay it between newspapers to dry.

SIMPLE PATTERNS WITH ACRYLIC MARBLING:

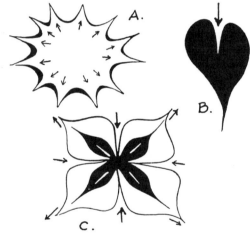

A. STARS - Drop the color on the size with an eye dropper. Then use a broom straw to start in the center and pull to the outside the number of points you want on the star.

B. HEARTS - Pull a straw straight across the diameter of the circle.

C. FLOWERS - Alternately pull the straw from the center to the outside, and from the outside to the center.

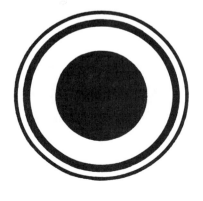

To get the concentric circles of different colors as used in A and C above drop each color in the center of the previous one. The outside rings will be the thinnest.

Bubble Marbling

Marbling does not have to be difficult or messy. Try this simple technique, which requires only a few supplies. Find a shallow dish or square pan that fits the dimensions of the card you want to use. Fill it with ½" water, and stir in several drops of bubble bath or dish soap. Instead of these, you can use undiluted commercial bubble-blowing solution made for children. Add a tablespoon or more of colored ink (marble a few test sheets to decide how much ink to use). Stick in the end of a drinking straw, and blow bubbles.

Lay a card or envelope on the bubbles to pick up the pattern. If parts of the pattern do not print, touch them up with watercolor or colored pencils. This marbling method works well on watercolor paper, which may be cut into postcards and package tags. Marble the edges of stationery. When doing envelopes, avoid ones made of shiny paper.

TO: *Gregory*
FROM: *Judith*

Sid Long
97 Q St.
Kidd, NY 08242

Happy Birthday

53

Paste Paper

The most interesting cards, envelopes, and wrappings are made from unusual paper. One simple way to decorate a plain sheet is to first brush it with a colored paste mixture. Then sweep the colors into patterns and let them dry. This is a little like finger painting, but with practice the results can be impressive.

HOMEMADE PASTE: Measure 4 cups of water and ¾ cup of sifted flour. Heat 3 cups of the water to a boil. Sprinkle the flour into the remaining cupful and mix it well to get rid of the lumps. Then stir it into the boiling water. Simmer it over medium heat for about 10 minutes, stirring constantly. After the paste thickens, strain it through a fine sieve, cool it, and pour into paper cups to add coloring. Gouache and tube watercolors need 2 tablespoons of Acrylic Matte Medium added to keep the paste from flaking off the paper when dry. Acrylic colors do not need the medium added. Store leftover paste in the refrigerator.

NO-COOK RECIPE: Combine 2 to 3 parts white library paste with one part diluted acrylic, watercolor, poster paint, or dye. Mix to the consistency of cream. Pour the mixture into the toe of a sheer nylon stocking and strain it by squeezing it through the nylon. This gets rid of the lumps. If the paste is too thick it will dry into mounds on the paper and later will flake off.

Making Paste Patterns

Wet the paper on both sides and smooth it down on a clean table or counter top. Brush on the paste with a wide brush, or pour a line of paste along an edge. Make patterns with combs, sponges, or anything that will make a design, including hands. If the pattern is not acceptable, crumple the paper and spread it out again. This makes an interesting random pattern. Lay the finished sheets on newspapers to dry or hang them on a clothes line. When they are dry, cut them into envelopes and liners, collage elements, package tags, wrapping paper, postcards, greeting cards, or greeting bags.

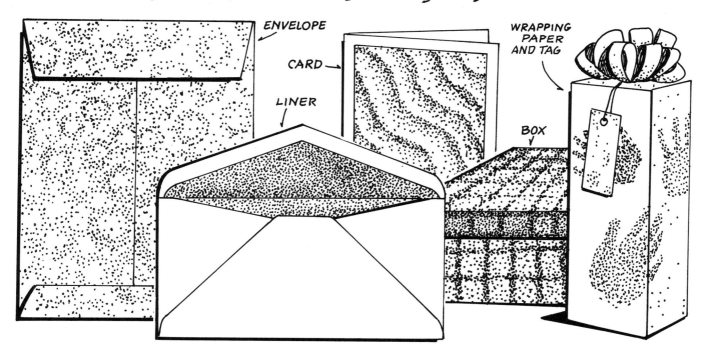

ENVELOPE

CARD

LINER

WRAPPING PAPER AND TAG

BOX

Wax Marbling

Marbling with wax is done by melting slivers of crayon onto simmering water, then laying paper down to pick up the pattern. Use a pan large enough for the paper and choose absorbent paper like construction, because the wax will pop off smooth surfaces.

Trim slivers of crayon into a saucer and crumble them with your fingers. Heat the pan of water to simmering, and turn off the heat. Sprinkle in the crayon pieces. Once they have melted, print immediately by rolling or laying the paper on the hot wax. The wax can be whipped into a finer pattern with a thin stick or broom straw. Remove the paper with tongs. It can be laid down again to double-print. Put the finished pieces between newspaper and place a board or weight on top so they will dry flat.

The marbled paper can be spray-mounted onto stiffer backing. Use them as mats around photos, or as paste-up elements in a collage. You also can tack down a silhouette to mask an area. Marble over the entire paper and then remove the mask.

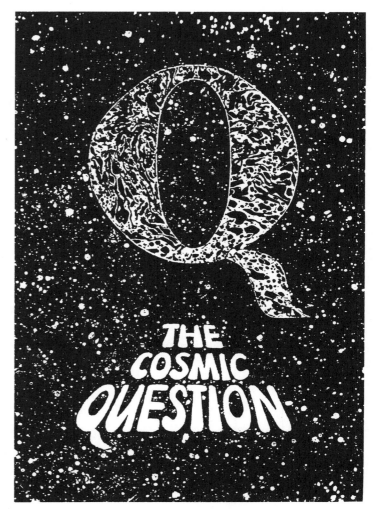

THIS GREETING CARD USES A WAX-MARBLED "Q" MOUNTED ON BLACK PAPER SPLATTERED WITH WHITE PAINT. THE QUESTION INSIDE COULD BE ANYTHING FROM "WILL YOU MARRY ME?" TO "IS THE CHECK IN THE MAIL YET?"

Fold-Dyeing

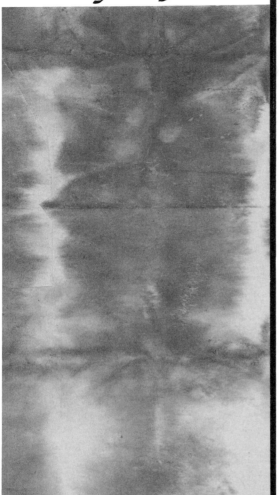

Fold-dyed paper is easy to make, and great for wrapping paper and matching cards, envelopes, and tags.

SUPPLIES:
* FOOD COLORING OR COLORED INKS
* RICE PAPER
* NEWSPAPER OR BLOTTING PAPER
* SHALLOW BOWLS

Directions: Saturate the rice paper in cold water and drain. Remove more water by pressing the sheets between newsprint or blotting paper. Handle the damp sheets carefully so as not to tear them. Use any folding variation: the more folds, the more complex the pattern. Dilute the food coloring or ink with water and put it in shallow bowls. Dip the edges and corners of the folded paper into the different colors. Open the paper and dry it flat.

Foil "Engraving"

Foil board comes in sheets the size of mat board. It is either silver or gold, and is almost mirror bright. The thin layer of foil, laminated onto its paper backing, makes the surface take impressions easily. When cut down to card size, the foil resembles a metallic plaque. "Engrave" on this by writing with the end of a darning needle stuck in a mat-knife handle, blunt-end up. Because the foil scratches easily, protect it with a cover sheet that doubles as a line guide. Use a script alphabet, and make the thick-and-thins in the letters by pressing lightly on up-strokes, and heavier on down-strokes. Remove the cover sheet to add descenders last. Illustrations and borders done in lines look good on this board, too. Glue your engraving to a greeting-card background, or fold it in half and make it serve as the card. The board's paper backing is white, so you can letter a message on it. Or use the foil board like a cover and put a page inside for the message. Make the foil look like a brass plaque by drawing the "screws" that hold the plaque in place. Put a circle in each corner, then cross the circles with lines. Engraved foil board also makes eye-catching package tags.

Foil Decorating

Foil comes on rolls, in many colors, and has a strip of plastic on the front that peels off after the foil is laid down. The foil sticks to an adhesive ground, and permanently adheres to wood, glass, plastic, and metal. Foil does not tarnish, and it gives a bright reflective finish.

Stir the liquid ground (also called size) instead of shaking the jar to minimize bubbles, which will mar the finished product.

Paint the ground on the area to be gilded with a brush or pen. Avoid leaving brush strokes that show up when dry. Clean your tools immediately afterward.

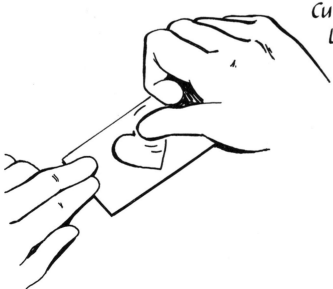

Cut a piece of foil to cover the ground. Lay the foil on the ground and burnish it down thoroughly with your thumbnail. Use your nail or a commercial burnisher to run around the edges for good contact. Remove the plastic facing and brush away excess foil.

More Shiny Stuff

Gouache itself comes in silver and gold – both in tubes and small pans of solid color that mix with water.

GOLD

Add a metallic luster to gouache and watercolor by mixing in metallic powder or mica crystals. They come in shades of gold and silver.

941 RICH GOLD METALLIC POWDER

MICA CRYSTALS

Pearlescent ink is found in many colors and gives sparkle to hand lettering and borders.

STARDUST NET. WT. 4.5 OZ

GLITTER COMES IN SHAKER-TOP TUBES AND IN SPRAYS.

Metallic thread and wire may be bought in spools to bind and decorate cards.

Metallic foil stars and hearts are backed with gum adhesive.

spray glitter SILVER

844 NEW PEARLY DEW

"NEW PEARLY DEW" GIVES CARDS AN OPALESCENT SHEEN

Thermography

Thermography is a four-step process that gives a raised, glossy image. Check Resources (page 133) for ordering clear stamp pad ink and resin.

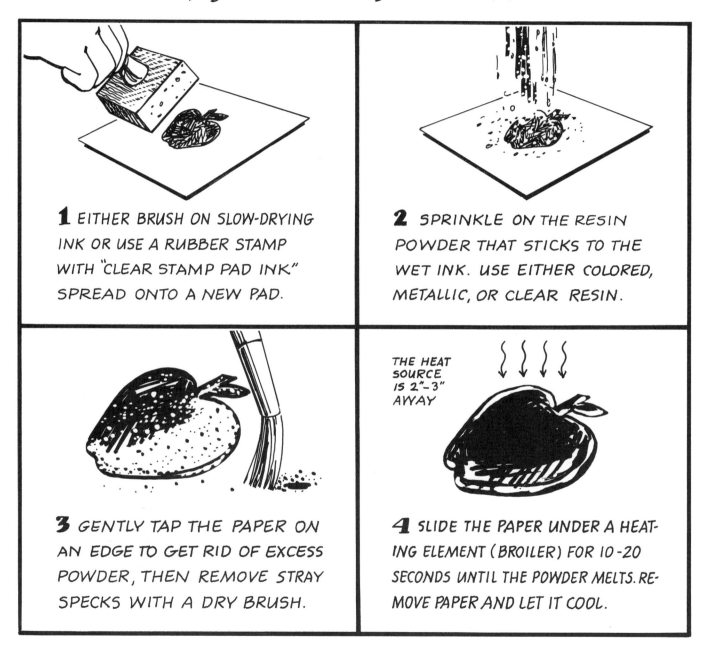

1 EITHER BRUSH ON SLOW-DRYING INK OR USE A RUBBER STAMP WITH "CLEAR STAMP PAD INK" SPREAD ONTO A NEW PAD.

2 SPRINKLE ON THE RESIN POWDER THAT STICKS TO THE WET INK. USE EITHER COLORED, METALLIC, OR CLEAR RESIN.

3 GENTLY TAP THE PAPER ON AN EDGE TO GET RID OF EXCESS POWDER, THEN REMOVE STRAY SPECKS WITH A DRY BRUSH.

THE HEAT SOURCE IS 2"-3" AWAY

4 SLIDE THE PAPER UNDER A HEATING ELEMENT (BROILER) FOR 10-20 SECONDS UNTIL THE POWDER MELTS. REMOVE PAPER AND LET IT COOL.

Gilding With Gold

The gilding process is this: Paint on a "ground" of gum ammoniac and let it dry. Use your breath to dampen it again. Then lay on it a piece of transfer gold and press it down firmly. Remove the gold's backing paper and cover the gold with a piece of glassine parchment. Burnish on top of the parchment to polish the gold. Remove the paper and brush away the excess. Supplies for gilding may be ordered from Pendragon (see Resources, page 133).

SUPPLIES:

* GUM AMMONIAC - PREPARE THE RESIN NODULES AS EXPLAINED TO THE RIGHT.
* GLASSINE PARCHMENT - THIS IS THE KIND OF PAPER IN WHICH COLLECTORS STORE POSTAGE STAMPS.
* SPOON BURNISHER - (LETRASET BRAND) THE BURNISHER SETS AND POLISHES THE GOLD.
* TRANSFER (PATENT) GOLD - IT COMES IN A BOOKLET OF SQUARE PIECES BACKED WITH PAPER.
* SCISSORS - THESE CUT THE GOLD
* BRUSH - USE A LARGE, SOFT BRUSH TO BRUSH AWAY THE EXCESS GOLD.

Gum Ammoniac~

BUY THIS IN NODULE FORM AND PREPARE IT IN THE STUDIO.

* GUM AMMONIAC NODULES
* DISTILLED WATER
* PINCH OF RED POWDERED PIGMENT
* TWO SMALL JARS
* OLD NYLON STOCKING
* DOUBLE BOILER

PUT THE NODULES IN A JAR AND COVER THEM WITH DISTILLED WATER. SOAK THEM OVERNIGHT. THEN HEAT THE JAR IN A DOUBLE BOILER, STIRRING UNTIL THE MIXTURE TURNS TO LIQUID. ADD A PINCH OF PIGMENT. STRAIN IT THROUGH A NYLON STOCKING SEVERAL TIMES, THEN STORE IT IN A CAPPED CLEAN JAR. WARM AND STIR THE GUM AMMONIAC BEFORE USING IT EACH TIME TO REDISTRIBUTE ANY SEDIMENT.

GUM AMMONIAC NODULES

1. LAYING THE GROUND

Warm and stir the gum ammoniac. Fill a pointed dip pen and outline the area to be gilded. Then flood the center. Work quickly because it dries fast. After it is dry, additional layers may be brushed on to build up height. Let the ground dry thoroughly. Gild the same day, or within a few days.

2. CLEANUP

Wash your hands and tools immediately with soap and hot water. Cleanser also helps. This ground is sticky and is hard on tools.

3. LAYING THE GOLD

Clean the scissor blades and cut a piece of gold to cover the design. Breathe on the ground as shown below to dampen it. Lay the gold on top and press it firmly with your fingers. Run a thumbnail around the edges. Remove the backing. Cover the design with glassine and burnish in various directions. Brush away the excess. Two layers of gold may be applied this way.

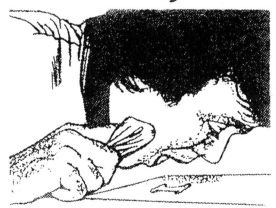

Language of Color

Color has its own special language. Here are a few important terms:

Hue — THE COLOR'S NAME: RED, BLUE, ETC.

Chroma — THE INTENSITY OR SATURATION OF A COLOR. TO DECREASE THE CHROMA IN A COLOR, MIX IT WITH ITS COMPLEMENTARY COLOR. IT WILL BRING IT CLOSER TO GRAY.

Complementary Colors — COLORS THAT ARE OPPOSITE EACH OTHER ON THE COLOR WHEEL.

Primary Colors — THESE CANNOT BE MADE BY MIXING OTHER COLORS. THEORETICALLY, THESE THREE, PLUS BLACK AND WHITE, ARE ALL YOU NEED TO CREATE ANY OTHER COLOR. THE PIGMENT PRIMARIES ARE RED (MAGENTA), BLUE (CYAN), AND YELLOW. A PRINTER USES ONLY MAGENTA, CYAN, YELLOW, AND BLACK INK TO CREATE ALL COLORS IN A PRINTED COLOR ILLUSTRATION.

Secondary Colors — COLORS MADE BY MIXING EQUAL AMOUNTS OF TWO PRIMARY COLORS (GREEN, ORANGE, AND VIOLET).

Tertiary Colors — COLORS MADE BY MIXING EQUAL AMOUNTS OF SECONDARY COLORS (RED-ORANGE, YELLOW-ORANGE, YELLOW-GREEN, BLUE-GREEN, BLUE-VIOLET, RED-VIOLET).

Monochromatic — COLOR SCHEME USING THE TINTS, TONES, AND SHADES FROM ONLY ONE HUE.

Achromatic — COLOR SCHEME USING ONLY BLACK AND GRAYS —AND WARM AND COOL WHITES.

Value — THE LIGHTNESS OR DARKNESS OF A COLOR. THE RELATIVE VALUE OF A COLOR IS FOUND BY USING A GRAY SCALE WITH HOLES PUNCHED IN IT: LAY IT OVER A COLOR AND SQUINT TO MAKE THE COLOR "DISAPPEAR."

Warm Colors — COLORS THAT CENTER AROUND ORANGE.

Cool Colors — COLORS THAT CENTER AROUND BLUE.

Tint — A COLOR THAT HAS WHITE MIXED IN IT.

Shade — A COLOR THAT HAS BLACK MIXED IN IT.

Tone — TONE RELATES TO GRAY AND APPLIES TO COLORS THAT HAVE THEIR COMPLEMENTARY COLORS ADDED.

Color: Gouache

Gouache is similar to watercolor in that it dilutes with water and requires the same tools and paper. It is, however, opaque. It has a medium-value color range that makes it difficult to mix very dark colors, but it produces some brilliant and high chroma hues. It is made of heavy pigment that is mixed in water to the consistency of cream. It does not work as a wash because it leaves a cloudy dull look.

Gouache can be thinned to use in a ruling pen for drawing line borders. It can also be used with a dip-nib calligraphy pen to make letters in color. Gouache's opacity is an advantage over colored ink because the color covers an area evenly. Ink tends to pool at the ends of strokes. Good brands of gouache include Winsor & Newton, Pelikan, and Talens. It comes in tubes and pans, and in metallic colors. The tube colors have about a two-year life span. Then they turn rock hard. The tubes can be broken open and the paint reconstituted by soaking it in distilled water.

Blending Colors–

FIRST, FILL IN THE IMAGE WITH MEDIUM VALUE COLORS.

ADD STROKES OF DARK VALUES FOR SHADED AREAS.

PAINT ON LIGHT HUES FOR THE HIGHLIGHTS.

WHEN DRY, BLEND THEM WITH A BRUSH AND CLEAN WATER.

A Flower For Each Month

COPY THE LINE DRAWING AND
COLOR IT AS SHOWN

January: Snowdrop

April: Daisy

February: Primrose

May: Hawthorn

March: Violet

June: Rose

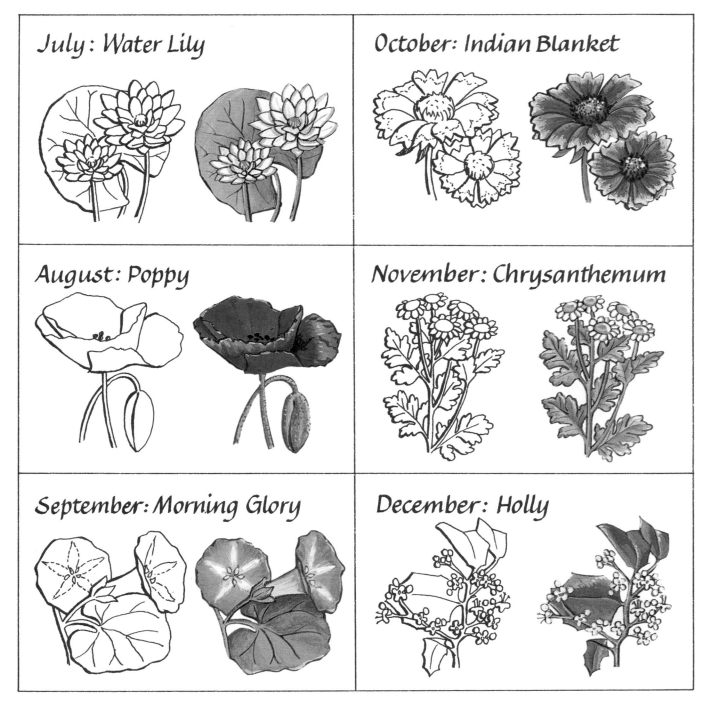

July: Water Lily

October: Indian Blanket

August: Poppy

November: Chrysanthemum

September: Morning Glory

December: Holly

Pressed Flowers

THIS PORTABLE FLOWER PRESS IS MADE FROM 5" X 5" MASONITE BOARD HELD TOGETHER BY BOLTS AND WING NUTS. CUT 10-12 SHEETS OF BLOTTING PAPER AND CLIP OFF THEIR CORNERS TO AVOID THE BOLTS.

Use dried flowers to decorate greeting cards. Take a flower press into the garden or field to press the flowers as they are picked. Choose from pansy, larkspur, coral bell, violas, and Queen Anne's Lace. Choose ones with radiating petals. Take apart some flowers to reassemble later. Remember to include some leaves and stalks. Look for samples among houseplants. Be sure to pack the press evenly so everything dries flat. Let the flowers dry from 1 to 2 weeks.

When you remove the petals, stems, and leaves, handle them with tweezers. Organize the layout before tacking the pieces down with a dot of stick glue on a toothpick. Cover the finished layout with a piece of clear Contact® paper.

Thinking of you

Marbled Paper Samples BY THOMAS LEECH, SAN MIGUEL PAPER WORKSHOP©

70

SAN MIGUEL PAPER WORKSHOP, 20 W. SAN MIGUEL, COLORADO SPRINGS, CO 80903 (PH. 719-635-9375)

Birth (Zodiac) Signs

USE THE SIGNS AND OTHER INFORMATION ON THIS CHART TO PERSONALIZE GREETING CARDS.

Solar Graphics

You can create silhouette illustrations with light-sensitive paper by laying objects on it, exposing it to sunlight, and developing the images. Solar Graphics®, P.O. Box 7091P, Berkeley, CA 94707, sells paper designed for this purpose. Lay the objects on the blue treated side and cover them with clear glass or plastic to hold them flat. Expose the paper to sunlight for 10 minutes. Then rinse the paper in a tray of tap water for 2-3 minutes. The images will be white on a blue background. Cut them apart for collage elements on cards.

Hole Punch Designs

Victorians used a hole-punching method to decorate greeting cards. The finished card was a beautiful lace-like design. The artist stacked and held together several cards to mass-produce them.

① Make a line drawing in pencil on the front of the pattern card. It can include lettering, borders, and illustration.

② Stack several blank cards beneath the pattern card, holding them together with bulldog clips or large paperclips.

③ Punch out the design by following the line drawing. Use a needle and thimble to punch small holes, and a pushpin for larger holes. Space the holes evenly. As a finishing touch, make a small punched design on the flaps or in the corners of the envelopes. (Note: Use this method to decorate package tags.)

CLAMP THE CARDS TOGETHER

Gyotaku

Gyotaku is Japanese fish printing. The raw fish is inked up and printed. It is a great way to send someone proof of your fish story, or to wish them one just as good.

DIRECTIONS: WASH AND DRY THE FISH. PLUG THE ORIFICES WITH PLASTICINE CLAY IF IT HAS ITS ENTRAILS INTACT. LAY THE FISH ON NEWSPAPER AND LEVEL ITS HEAD AND TAIL WITH CHUNKS OF CLAY UNDER THEM. FLARE THE FINS AND STICK STRAIGHT PINS THROUGH THEM DEEP ENOUGH TO NOT INTERFERE WITH THE PRINTING. MIX PRINT-MAKING INK IN A SAUCER AND PAINT IT ON THE FISH. SMOOTH THE STROKES WITH A DRY BRUSH. LAY RICE PAPER ON THE FISH AND PRESS FROM THE MIDDLE OUT TO PICK UP THE IMAGE. WHEN THE PRINT IS DRY, PAINT THE EYE AND ADD WASHES FOR SHADOWS AND COLOR.

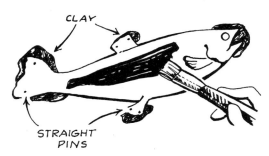

CLAY

STRAIGHT PINS

PRESS FROM THE MIDDLE OUT TO PRINT

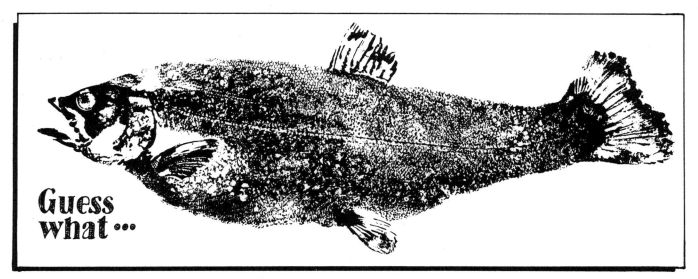

Guess what ...

PRINT THE FISH ON THE CARD'S COVER AND WRITE THE DETAILS OF A "FISH STORY" INSIDE.

Quilling

Quilling paper comes in narrow strips in many colors. Buy it in craft stores. The paper is wound and curled into shapes that are glued to cards, envelopes, packages, and package tags.

USE A DARNING NEEDLE STUCK IN A CORK WITH THE TIP OF THE EYE CLIPPED OFF TO HOLD THE PAPER.

10"x10" CARDBOARD COVERED WITH WAXED PAPER FOR A WORK SURFACE.

PAPER RINGS ABOUT 1" IN DIAMETER.

TOOTHPICKS

GLUE STICK

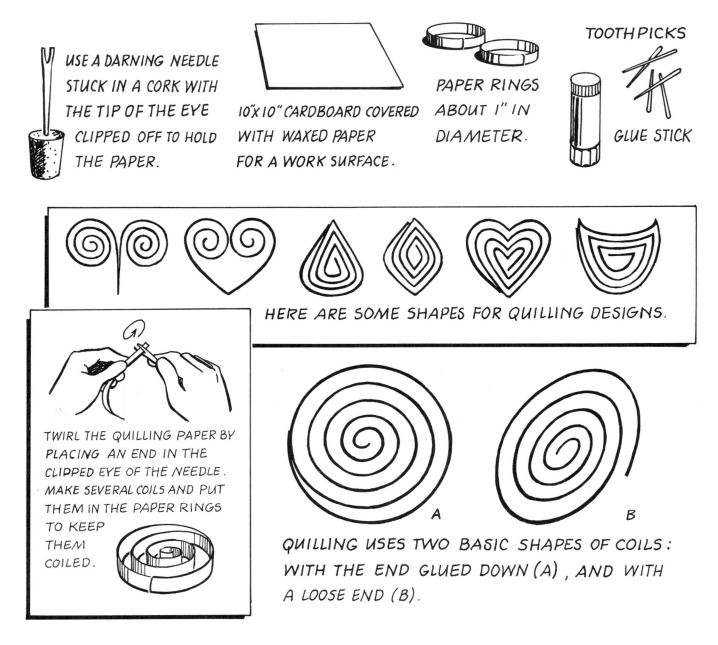

HERE ARE SOME SHAPES FOR QUILLING DESIGNS.

TWIRL THE QUILLING PAPER BY PLACING AN END IN THE CLIPPED EYE OF THE NEEDLE. MAKE SEVERAL COILS AND PUT THEM IN THE PAPER RINGS TO KEEP THEM COILED.

A

B

QUILLING USES TWO BASIC SHAPES OF COILS: WITH THE END GLUED DOWN (A), AND WITH A LOOSE END (B).

COILS

 COIL THE PAPER TIGHTLY AND GLUE DOWN THE END BY DABBING ON THE GLUE WITH A TOOTHPICK WHILE THE COIL IS TIGHT. USE THIS FOR THE CENTER OF FLOWERS.

 LOOSEN THE COIL BEFORE GLUE-ING THE END FOR LARGE SPIRALS.

 MAKE PETALS AND OTHER SHAPES BY PINCHING THE COIL TOGETHER IN DIFFERENT PLACES. EXPERIMENT WITH NEW SHAPES, OR USE THE ONES SUGGESTED ON THE PREVIOUS PAGE.

SCROLLS

 A MAKE A SCROLL BY CURLING THE ENDS IN OPPOSITE DIREC-TIONS (A), OR THE SAME B DIRECTION (B). VARY THE NUMBER OF TWISTS AND THE LENGTH OF THE PAPER FOR DIFFERENT SIZES.

 THE FIRST TWO SHAPES TO THE LEFT ARE MADE FROM A SCROLL CURLED LIKE "B" ABOVE, AND PINCHED.

 THE BOTTOM TENDRIL SHAPE IS FROM A SCROLL CURLED LIKE "A" ABOVE, AND PINCHED.

Thinking of You

Celtic Patterns

Celtic patterns can be used on cards and envelopes. Make a design into a rubber stamp to decorate wrapping paper, or emboss the design.

CELTIC INTERLACING IS MADE BY USING A GRID FOR THE STRUCTURE OF THE DESIGN.

① MARK DOTS ON THE GRID IN TWO DIF- FERENT COLORS, REPEATING A FIVE-DOT PATTERN.

② START ANYWHERE AND DRAW SHORT DIAGONAL LINES FROM ONE COLORED DOT TO THE SECOND COLOR, KEEPING INSIDE THE DOTS.

③ ADD DIAGONAL LINES IN THE OPPOSITE DIRECTION TO ESTABLISH THE WEAVE.

④ CONTINUE THE PATTERN OVERALL AND CONNECT THE EDGES TO FINISH.

SQUARE   TRIANGLE   CIRCLE

ABOVE—THREE KNOT SHAPES. THE SQUARE AND CIRCLE USE THE GRID.

SPIRALS ARE CLASSIC CELTIC DESIGNS. THEY ARE NOT DIFFICULT TO MAKE.

Ⓐ MAPPING A TWO-BAND SPIRAL.

Ⓑ MAPPING A THREE-BAND SPIRAL.

ABOVE—SPIRAL BORDER.

RIGHT— THREE SPIRAL GROUPS.

Heraldry

Give an historic and traditional look to a greeting card by using elements of heraldry in the design. There are nine parts to heraldic arms, as shown below. These may be used in different combinations, or alone. (Reference : <u>Design</u> <u>Your</u> <u>Own</u> <u>Coat</u> <u>of</u> <u>Arms</u> by Rosemary A. Chorzempa, Dover Publications, 1987).

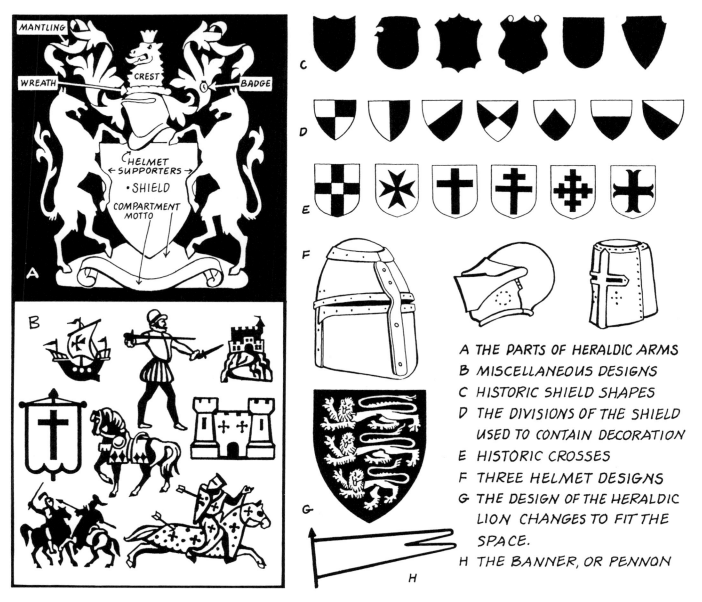

A THE PARTS OF HERALDIC ARMS

B MISCELLANEOUS DESIGNS

C HISTORIC SHIELD SHAPES

D THE DIVISIONS OF THE SHIELD USED TO CONTAIN DECORATION

E HISTORIC CROSSES

F THREE HELMET DESIGNS

G THE DESIGN OF THE HERALDIC LION CHANGES TO FIT THE SPACE.

H THE BANNER, OR PENNON

Brush Flowers

Paint these flowers with a Japanese calligraphy brush and watercolor. You might also use a brush-tipped marker.

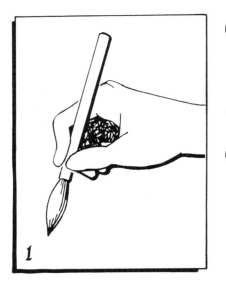

① Hold the brush upright. It may be either well-loaded or slightly dry.

② Make teardrop petals by pulling the brush along its axis. Raise and lower it to get pointed ends. Rotate the art.

SUGGESTION: Dip the brush into two colors before making the petals so they blend on the page. Or paint the petals with clear water, then flood them with color from another brush. After the petals dry, you might stroke on a secondary wash for shading. Define them further with dark veins and shadows for contrast.

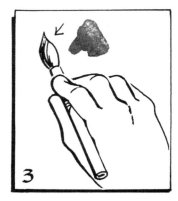

③ Make asymmetrical leaves and petals by pressing down the brush and pulling to the side as shown.

CHANGE PRESSURE AND DIRECTION.

Texture

Above: Use a sponge to make letters through a template, or make the letters out of sponge and print them one at a time. Below: Mask off the edges of a layout and make a sponge border using a natural sponge.

Carnival ⊤ decorative webbing is available in several colors and comes in spray cans. Carnival⊤ treated paper makes interesting wrapping paper, or cut it into paste-up elements for cards.

Below: Add texture to letters by notching them with gouache that matches the color of the paper.

Halloween

Below: Lay paper on stone and use a crayon or colored pencil to rub background texture on a card.

More Ideas

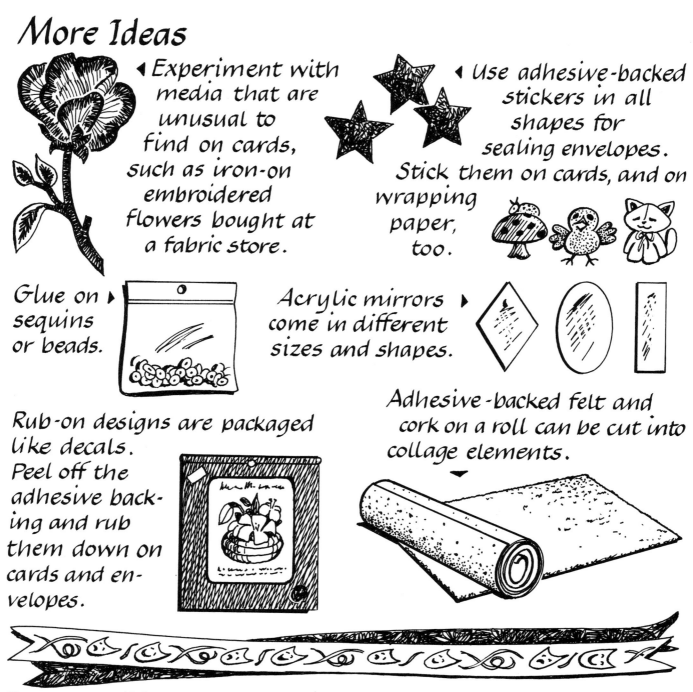

◄ Experiment with media that are unusual to find on cards, such as iron-on embroidered flowers bought at a fabric store.

◄ Use adhesive-backed stickers in all shapes for sealing envelopes. Stick them on cards, and on wrapping paper, too.

Glue on ▸ sequins or beads.

Acrylic mirrors ▸ come in different sizes and shapes.

Rub-on designs are packaged like decals. Peel off the adhesive backing and rub them down on cards and envelopes.

Adhesive-backed felt and cork on a roll can be cut into collage elements.

Decorator ribbons are available in many widths. They have a variety of designs, and make great borders or bands of designs on cards. Use them on the gift wrapping, too.

ENVELOPES

Buying and Making Envelopes

Visit local wholesale paper supply houses to find a variety of envelopes, and to get sample booklets. Here are some standard sizes for envelopes:

3 7/8″ X 7 1/2″   4 1/8″ X 9 1/2″ (※10)
  (Monarch)   4 3/4″ X 6 1/2″ (A6)
4 3/8″ X 5 3/4 (A2)   5 1/4″ X 7 1/4″ (A7)

Do not buy coated paper because the coating repels ink and paint. Test your media on the booklet samples to see how it looks.

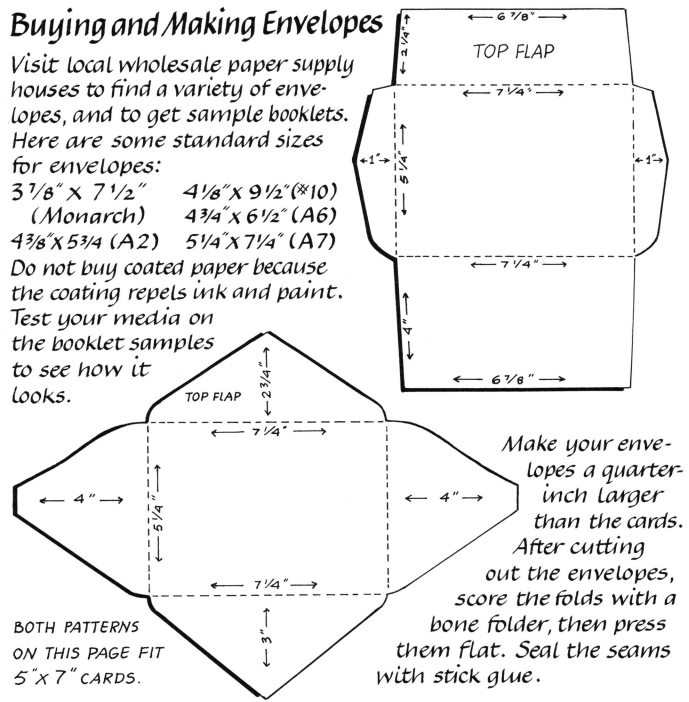

TOP FLAP

6 7/8″

2 1/4″

7 1/4″

1″   5 1/4″   1″

7 1/4″

4″

6 7/8″

TOP FLAP

2 3/4″

7 1/4″

4″   5 1/4″   4″

7 1/4″

3″

BOTH PATTERNS ON THIS PAGE FIT 5″X 7″ CARDS.

Make your envelopes a quarter-inch larger than the cards. After cutting out the envelopes, score the folds with a bone folder, then press them flat. Seal the seams with stick glue.

Use glue stick, sealing wax or decorative stickers to seal the envelopes. You might also make your own glue: Mix a tablespoon of white glue with a tablespoon of vinegar.

Add a drop of peppermint flavoring. Brush it onto the flap and let it dry. Lick and seal them as you would any commercially made envelope.

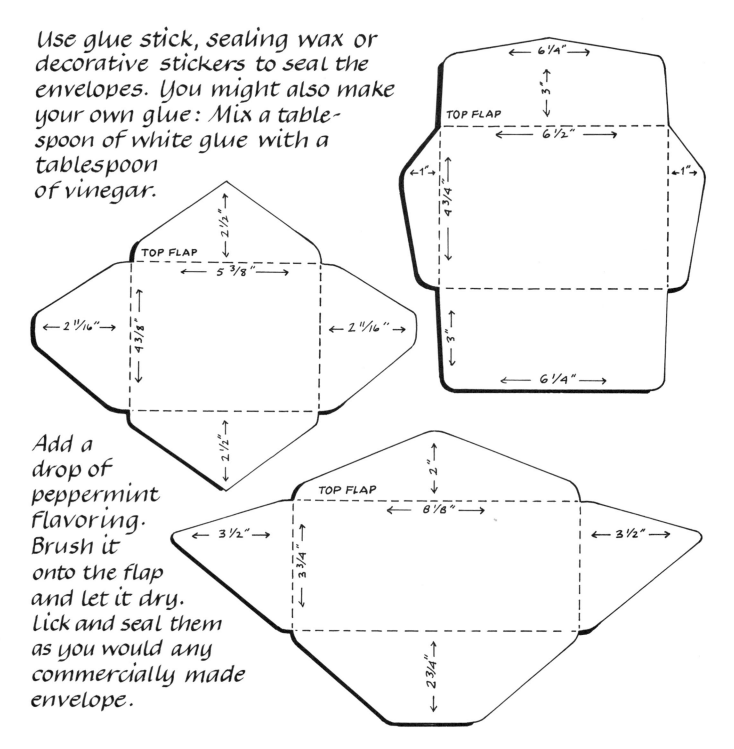

Card Without an Envelope

Use card stock. Score the fold lines, fold them, and burnish the folds. Open the card and write the greeting inside, then fold the flaps down as shown. They will hold themselves closed.

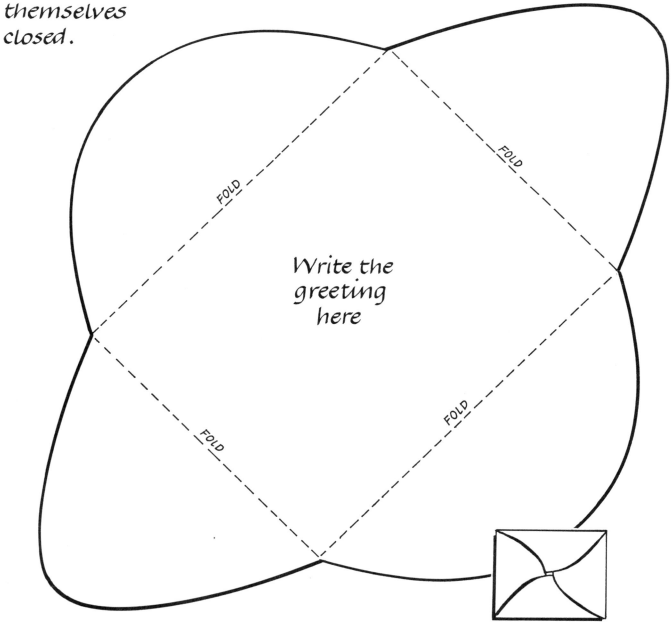

FOLD

FOLD

FOLD

FOLD

Write the greeting here

Addressing Envelopes

There are several ways to address envelopes, depending on how many you need and the type of paper from which they are made. Choose envelopes with a smooth, but not shiny, surface. Sacrifice at least one for practice. Draw three or four base lines on it in pencil, erasing if you need to relocate the lines for optimum appearance. Test different pens and lettering styles on a sample address to find the right combination.

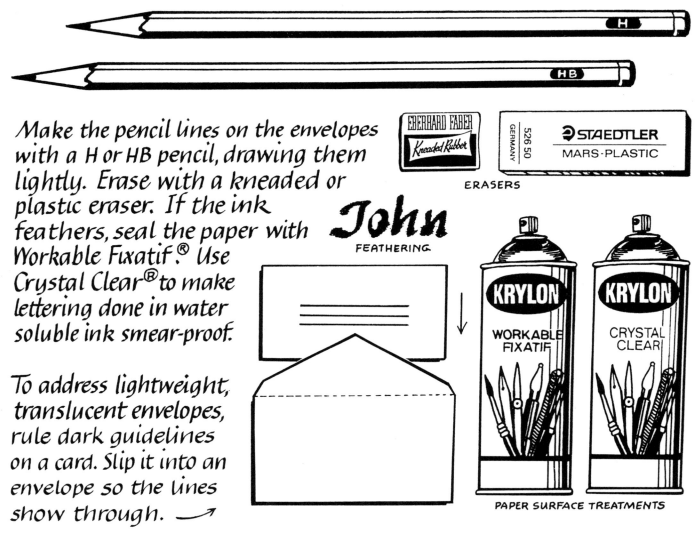

Make the pencil lines on the envelopes with a H or HB pencil, drawing them lightly. Erase with a kneaded or plastic eraser. If the ink feathers, seal the paper with Workable Fixatif.® Use Crystal Clear® to make lettering done in water soluble ink smear-proof.

To address lightweight, translucent envelopes, rule dark guidelines on a card. Slip it into an envelope so the lines show through. ⟶

ERASERS

John
FEATHERING

KRYLON
WORKABLE FIXATIF

KRYLON
CRYSTAL CLEAR

PAPER SURFACE TREATMENTS

Use the following methods for addressing heavier envelopes and ones with liners.

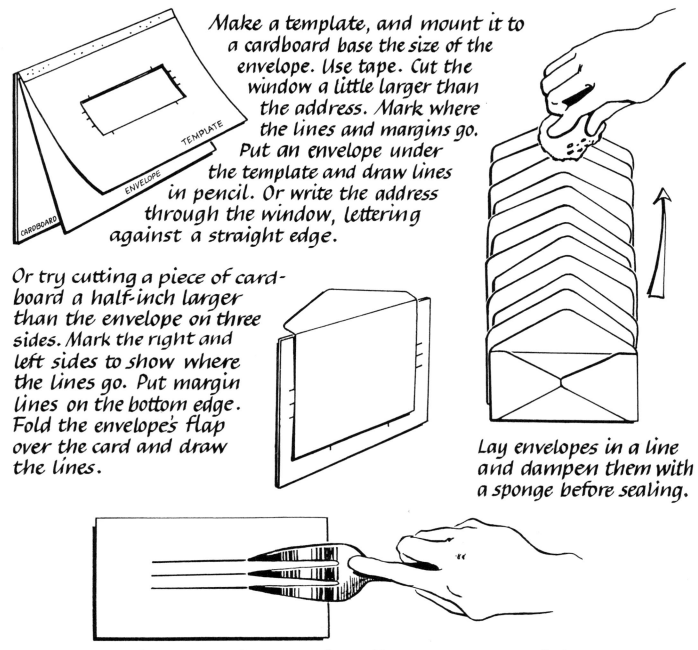

Make a template, and mount it to a cardboard base the size of the envelope. Use tape. Cut the window a little larger than the address. Mark where the lines and margins go. Put an envelope under the template and draw lines in pencil. Or write the address through the window, lettering against a straight edge.

Or try cutting a piece of cardboard a half-inch larger than the envelope on three sides. Mark the right and left sides to show where the lines go. Put margin lines on the bottom edge. Fold the envelope's flap over the card and draw the lines.

Lay envelopes in a line and dampen them with a sponge before sealing.

Another method is to score lines with a large 3-prong fork.

Address Labels

Personal address labels make good gifts to friends. Or use them on your own correspondence as a way of identifying you with your style. Take the artwork to a quick printer that can print them on adhesive-backed labels.

Consider having labels printed on colored foil or clear acetate that has an adhesive backing. Commercial printers can also make labels in nonstandard sizes.

Draw the artwork and lettering in black ink on a blue-lined grid to keep the layout squared. Work within an area that measures 4½" wide by 1⅜" tall. Use calligraphy or press-on letters. Put the complete address on either 3 or 4 lines, and avoid very thin strokes, because this layout should be

reduced 33% to measure 2" x 5/8". Thin strokes tend to disappear when reduced. Add monograms, decorated letters, borders, or other bold artwork.

Titles for Addressing Envelopes

Married Couple:
MR. AND MRS. JOHN SMITH

Couple Living Together:
(USE ONE LINE FOR EACH NAME)
MS. JANE DOE
MR. JOHN SMITH

Wife Uses Maiden Name:
MR. JOHN SMITH AND MS. JANE DOE

Divorced Woman:
MRS. JANE SMITH, OR
MRS. DOE-SMITH (MAIDEN AND MARRIED NAME)
MRS. JANE DOE (RESTORED MAIDEN NAME)

Widowed Woman:
MRS. JOHN SMITH; MRS. JANE SMITH

Married — Both With Titles:
THE DOCTORS SMITH, OR
DR. JOHN SMITH AND DR. JANE SMITH

Only The Wife Has A Title:
(THE TITLED PERSON IS LISTED FIRST)
DR. JANE SMITH AND MR. JOHN SMITH

Clergy:
PROTESTANT: (MALE MINISTER) THE REVEREND AND MRS. HENRY JONES; (FEMALE MINISTER) THE REVEREND MARY JONES AND MR. HENRY JONES

CATHOLIC:
POPE: HIS HOLINESS POPE JOHN
CARDINAL: HIS EMINENCE HENRY JONES
BISHOP: THE MOST REVEREND HENRY JONES
PRIEST: THE REVEREND FATHER HENRY JONES
SISTER: SISTER MARY (ADD INITIALS OF ORDER)
BROTHER: BROTHER JAMES (INITIALS OF ORDER)

JEWISH:
RABBI AND MRS. HENRY JONES, OR
DR. AND MRS. HENRY JONES (IF THE RABBI HAS A DOCTORATE)

"The Honorable" is used on high-ranking American officials such as ambassadors, judges, commissioners, attorney generals, state congressmen, etc.

Use "Ms." when a woman's marital status is unknown, when she asks that it be used, or when addressing a professional woman. Acceptable abbreviations include Mr., Mrs., Dr., Jr., and military titles. The abbreviation Jr. or II, which shows a person has the same name as his father, is preceded by a comma.

FORMAT AND THEME CARDS

Reminder Knot

This clever reminder knot is easy to make. It can be glued to a card, a letter, or a gift box. Make it out of colored paper. Because the message is written on only one side, you can reproduce it on a photocopier and attach knots to several cards.

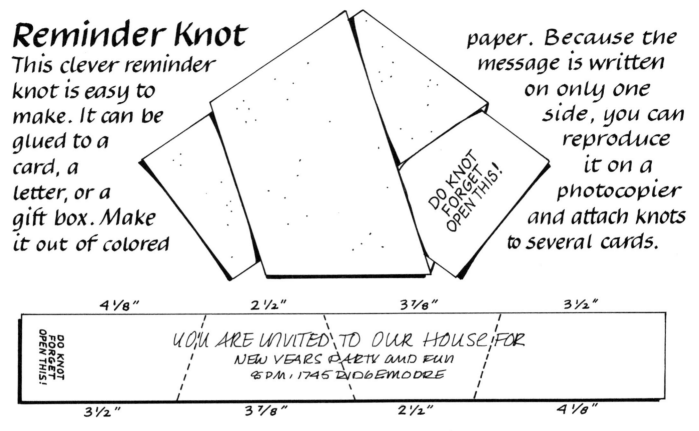

The strip of paper measures 14" x 2," and is folded three times. Write the message horizontally on one side, and locate the reminder within an inch of the left end. Leave at least another inch of blank space as the left margin on the quote.

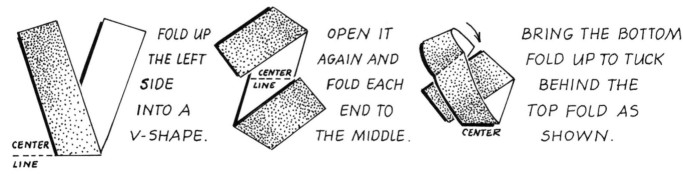

FOLD UP THE LEFT SIDE INTO A V-SHAPE.

OPEN IT AGAIN AND FOLD EACH END TO THE MIDDLE.

BRING THE BOTTOM FOLD UP TO TUCK BEHIND THE TOP FOLD AS SHOWN.

Scroll Card

SUPPLIES:

* BAMBOO SKEWER OR 1/8" DIAMETER DOWEL
* 2 WOODEN BEADS WITH 1/8" DIAMETER HOLES
* 15" X 3" PAPER WITH THE GRAIN ACROSS IT
* 10" PIECE OF 1/4" WIDE RIBBON
* GLUE
* MAT KNIFE

CUT A 3½" PIECE OF BAMBOO BY ROTATING IT UNDER A KNIFE BLADE TO SCORE IT BEFORE BREAKING IT. SAND THE ENDS SMOOTH.

GLUE THE WOODEN BEADS TO THE ENDS. LET DRY.

DECORATE THE SCROLL, LEAVING THE TOP 1½" AND THE BOTTOM 3½" BLANK.

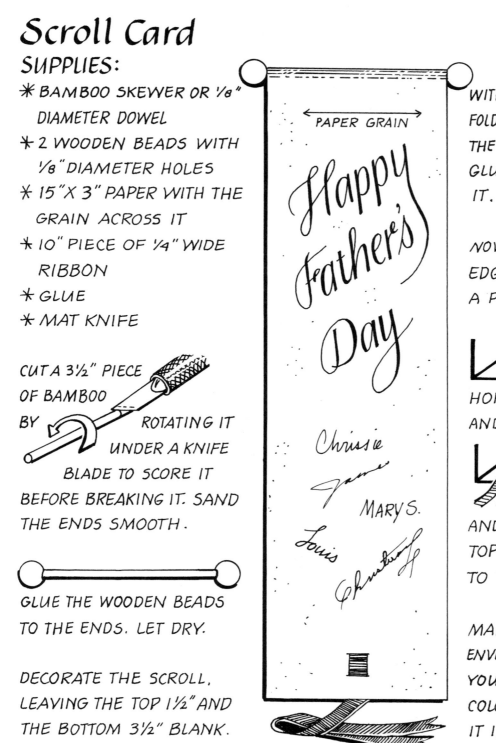

PAPER GRAIN

Happy Father's Day

Chrissie
Jane
MARY S.
Louis
Christoph

WITH THE BACK FACING UP FOLD THE TOP OF THE PAPER OVER THE BAMBOO ROD ½" AND GLUE IT.

NOW FOLD THE BOTTOM EDGE INTO A POINT.

THEN FOLD IT UP AND GLUE IT. CUT HORIZONTAL SLITS 3/8" WIDE AND THREAD THE RIBBON THROUGH THEM. TURN OVER THE SCROLL AND ROLL IT UP FROM THE TOP. USE THE RIBBON TO TIE IT CLOSED.

MAIL THE SCROLL IN A SMALL ENVELOPE MADE FOR THANK-YOU NOTES. OR WRAP IT IN COLORED TISSUE AND MAIL IT IN A TUBE.

Accordion-Fold Card

To make a simple accordion-fold card decide on the finished size, for example 5"x7". Multiply the width by the number of folds to get the proportions for the paper. Measure and fold the card carefully. Be sure to burnish the folds flat.

FRONT COVER

The card to the right is made from a piece of paper measuring 20 inches wide and 7 inches tall. It is folded into four sections.

The first three sections have their tops cut out along the line of the illustration. So when it is closed, the card looks as it does here. (Only the buildings make up the cover and are cut out along the skyline.) The illustrations on the inside are shown on the next page.

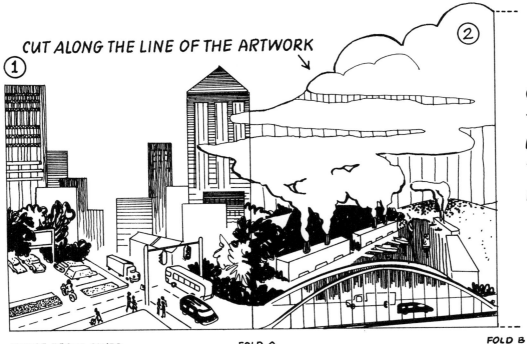

CUT ALONG THE LINE OF THE ARTWORK

① ②

THIS EDGE
CONNECTS
TO THE LEFT
EDGE OF
THE SECTIONS
BELOW

INSIDE FRONT COVER   FOLD A   FOLD B

ON THE CARD
THE MINI VAN
IS SHOWN
LEAVING THE
CITY, CROSSING
THE BRIDGE
TO THE
COUNTRY,
THEN TRAVEL-
ING UP THE
MOUNTAINS.

③ ④

HAVE A
GREAT
VACATION!

FOLD B   FOLD C   INSIDE BACK COVER

93

Hearts

MAKE A HEART BANNER BY CUTTING INIVIDUAL HEARTS OF THE SAME OR DIFFERENT SIZES FROM COLORED PAPER. CUT THEM ON A FOLD AS SHOWN. HANG AND TAPE THEM ON COLORED YARN.

DOUBLE-SIDED TAPE

MAKE WOVEN HEARTS FROM TWO COLORS OF FOIL, WRAPPING PAPER, OR COLORED PAPER. CUT EACH SIDE FROM A 2"X6" PIECE OF PAPER FOLDED IN HALF, AND MAKE ½" X 2" SLITS FOR WEAVING.

REPEAT THIS HEART FOR EMBOSSING, SCREEN PRINTING, STAMPING, MAKING CUT-OUTS, OR PAINTING.

TRACE AND PAINT THIS HEART BORDER. CUT OUT THE MIDDLE FOR A WINDOW TO FRAME QUILTING, A PHOTO, OR RIBBON WEAVING.

Doll Chain Card

DESIGN A SILHOUETTE FOR YOUR CARD THAT CONNECTS AT LEAST TWO PLACES ON THE RIGHT AND LEFT EDGES. FAN-FOLD MEDIUM-WEIGHT PAPER. PRESS THE FOLDS FLAT WITH A PAPER FOLDER. HOLD THE STACK CLOSED WITH BULLDOG CLIPS WHILE YOU CUT THROUGH THE LAYERS WITH A MAT KNIFE OR SCISSORS.

Name Tag Cards

MEASURE THE WIDTH OF THE ROUND BUTTON TAG AND CUT A CIRCLE IN THE CARD'S FRONT COVER, USING A TEMPLATE. MAKE A SLIT BETWEEN TWO SMALL HOLES AS SHOWN ON THE INSIDE OF THE CARD. PUSH THE CLOSED PIN ON THE BACK OF THE BUTTON THROUGH IT.

IF THE NAME TAGS ARE PAPER WITH A BACKING, PUT THEM IN A POCKET CARD (SEE PAGE 101). PUT RECTANGULAR PLASTIC TAGS INSIDE THE CARD WITH THE CLOSED PIN PUSHED THROUGH A SLIT.

Wind Greeting

These greetings are made on strips of brown paper hung from trees. Passers-by first see the strips spinning in the wind, then investigate to find a cheerful sentiment. They must be removed in a few days.

Hang them with string or twine. Several people can make this a group project by hanging them outside the window of a sick friend's room, or from the ceiling of a co-worker's office.

Cut 3"x10" pieces from brown paper grocery sacks. Turn down one end about 2". Punch a hole for the string or twine. Write a blessing, greeting, or short inspirational poem of 10 to 12 words. Do this in ink, acrylic, or poster paint. Draw a large question mark on one side, and the quote on the other. Hang wind greetings in the evening to give the recipient an early morning surprise.

Never-Ending Card

This card is in a booklet format, with sewn or stapled pages. Read it from front to back. Then turn it over to discover another front cover. Read it front to back, turn it over, and you are at the beginning again. Whatever sentiment is expressed inside never ends.

COVER
PAGES
TOP VIEW

Cut a cover three times the booklet's width. For a 5"x7" booklet it would be 15"x7". Fold it zig-zag into thirds and decorate the covers. Cut the desired number of 9½"x7" pages, and fold them in half. Stack them, write the message, and staple or bind them in the booklet as shown below.

SUGGESTIONS: The covers can be the same or different, but the concept should be able to start from either end. For example, illustrate a disaster of some kind on the front cover, like a sofa shredded by a cat, with a turned over litter pan on the back cover. Or a teenager's party mess, followed by an empty six-pack on the back cover— and write "Welcome Home." Then rubber-stamp footprints, pawprints, or whatever is appropriate throughout the booklet. The prints never end, so the reader never catches the culprit.

BINDING

USE A BOOKBINDER'S STAPLER. OR PUNCH THREE HOLES AND SEW THE PAGES.

TIE KNOT AND CLIP

Tree Ornament Card

Cut on the solid lines, and fold on the dotted lines. Seal the flaps with a glue stick.

Loop a string over this tab and glue down the tab to hang on a Christmas tree.

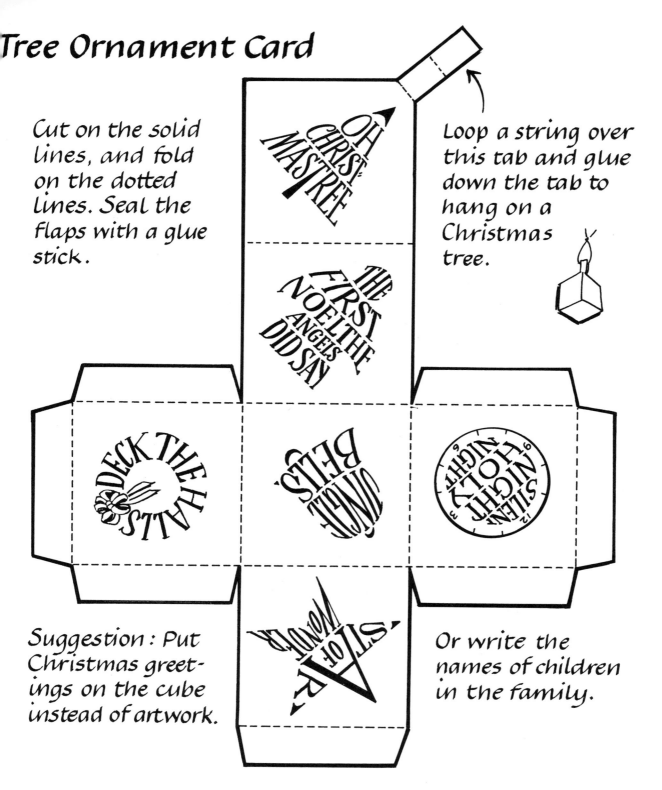

Suggestion: Put Christmas greetings on the cube instead of artwork.

Or write the names of children in the family.

Möbius Strip

This greeting is amazing for its simplicity and originality. It is another way to express a never-ending sentiment. A 19th-century German mathematician named August Möbius invented the strip. It is a piece of paper glued into a twisted ring that seems to have only one side.

FLIP TOWARD YOU TO FINISH THE QUOTE

Hang the ring over a door-knob for the right person to discover. Give it in a small box as a bracelet whose sentiment is more valuable than the object. Or hang it on a Christmas tree.

---

① CUT A LENGTHY ½" WIDE STRIP OF PAPER. LEAVE A BLANK SPACE FOR GLUE AND LETTER A QUOTE. CUT OFF THE EXCESS PAPER, LEAVING ANOTHER BLANK SPACE FOR GLUE:

② FLIP THE PAPER OVER TOWARD YOU AND CONTINUE THE QUOTE, OR REPEAT THE FIRST ONE. DO NOT LEAVE A PLACE FOR GLUE. LETTER IN A DIFFERENT COLOR TO PROVE YOU STARTED WITH TWO SIDES.

③ APPLY STICK GLUE TO THE BLANK ENDS AND TWIST THE STRIP TO JOIN THEM. FEED THE PAPER THROUGH YOUR FINGERS AS YOU READ IT. THE QUOTE IS CONTINUOUS.

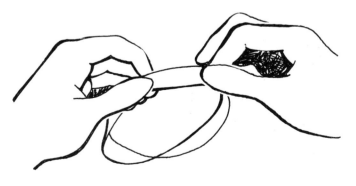

Tent Cards

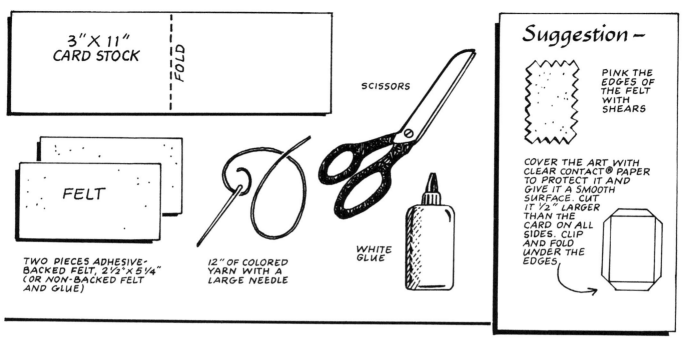

3" X 11" CARD STOCK — FOLD

FELT

TWO PIECES ADHESIVE-BACKED FELT, 2½" X 5¼" (OR NON-BACKED FELT AND GLUE)

12" OF COLORED YARN WITH A LARGE NEEDLE

SCISSORS

WHITE GLUE

Suggestion —

PINK THE EDGES OF THE FELT WITH SHEARS

COVER THE ART WITH CLEAR CONTACT® PAPER TO PROTECT IT AND GIVE IT A SMOOTH SURFACE. CUT IT ½" LARGER THAN THE CARD ON ALL SIDES. CLIP AND FOLD UNDER THE EDGES

Tent cards convey greetings, as do other cards, but end up decorating desks and tables. Cut the card from 3"x11" card stock. Fold it in half and decorate it as shown with calligraphy, dried flowers, watercolor, ribbon, and so on. Next, cut the felt lining — two pieces measuring 2½" X 5¼". Thread the yarn in the needle and punch it through each piece of felt ½" from its lower edge. Knot the back and anchor it with a dot of white glue. (Note: Leave about 3" of yarn between the felts.) Position the adhesive-backed felts inside the card and press them flat. (Use glue if they are not adhesive-backed.)

DRAW THE ARTWORK END TO END

THE FELTS, SHOWING THE KNOTS AND YARN

Pocket Card

This pocket, glued to the front of a card, can hold small gifts of money, jewelry, pressed flowers, a love note, or whatever. Hand-decorate the paper for the pocket, or use anything from foil to wrapping paper. Leave the last flap unfolded.

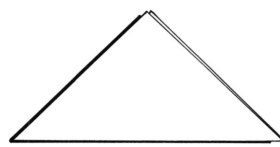

START WITH A SQUARE OF PAPER 4"X 4" OR 6"X 6" AND FOLD IT IN HALF TO MAKE A TRIANGLE.

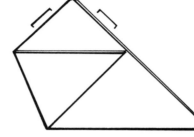

FOLD THE LEFT POINT TO THE RIGHT SO THE TRIANGLE AT TOP HAS TWO EQUAL SIDES.

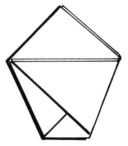

FOLD THE RIGHT POINT AS SHOWN.

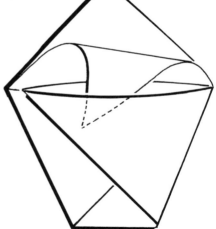

FOLD ONE TOP FLAP INTO THE BODY OF THE NEAR TRIANGLE TO FINISH THE POCKET.

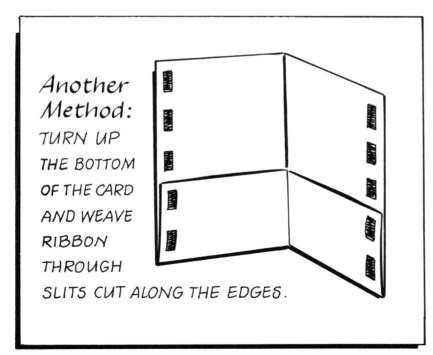

Another Method: TURN UP THE BOTTOM OF THE CARD AND WEAVE RIBBON THROUGH SLITS CUT ALONG THE EDGES.

Vellum Pockets

These beautiful vellum pockets may be slipped inside another card, or sent alone. The vellum flaps fold over each other to make a flower or star pattern when the light shines through. Put delicate dried flowers between two layers of vellum tracing paper to add color and shadows. You can also put a message card inside (also made of vellum). The pocket's flaps do not need glue.

LAY TWO PIECES OF VELLUM ON THE PATTERN AND TRACE.

NOTCH AND TRIM THE PAPER BETWEEN THE FLAPS. FOLD AND BURNISH ON THE DOTTED LINES.

INSERT THE FLOWERS BETWEEN THE SHEETS.

LAY THE MESSAGE CARD ON TOP AND TUCK IN THE FLAPS OVER IT.

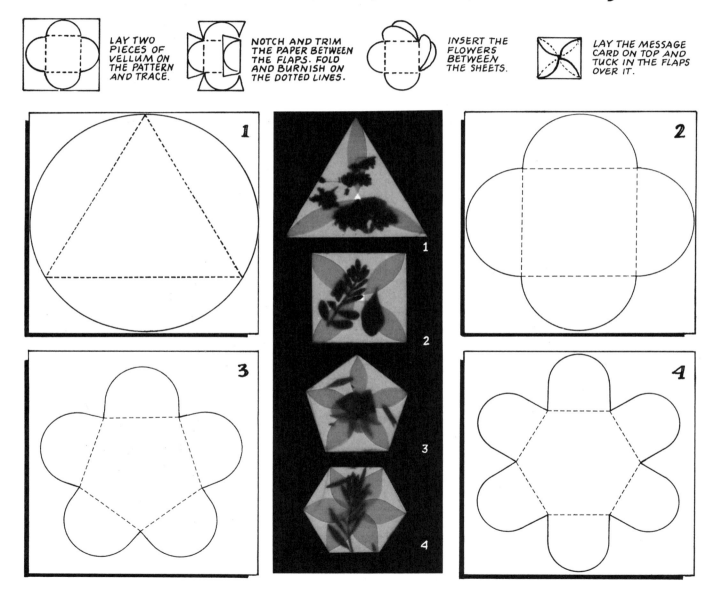

Movable Cards
FAN CARD

CUT 5, 7, OR 9 PIECES OF CARD STOCK SHAPED LIKE ONE SECTION OF A FAN. DECORATE THEM, AND HOLD THEM TOGETHER WITH A BRASS BRAD.

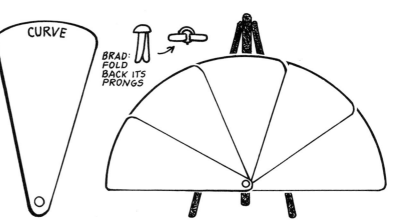

THE ORDER IN WHICH THE SECTIONS ARE STACKED MAKES THE FAN OPEN CORRECTLY

SELECTOR CARD

DIVIDE A CIRCLE INTO SECTIONS AND DECORATE EACH ONE. FOLD A CARD AS SHOWN. NOTCH ONE EDGE AND PUT THE CIRCLE IN THE LAST FOLD. ATTACH IT WITH A BRAD. GLUE THE LAST FOLD SHUT. TURN THE CIRCLE THROUGH THE NOTCH TO SHOW SELECTIONS THROUGH THE CUT-OUT WINDOWS.

PULL TAB

FOLD THE CARD AS ABOVE. CUT THE WINDOWS, AND NOTCH THE BOT-TOM EDGE. DRAW THE PULL-TAB ART ON PAPER SLIGHTLY NARROWER THAN THE WIDTH OF THE CARD. POSITION IT INSIDE THE LAST FOLD. GLUE THE EDGES OF THE FOLD, BUT LET THE INSERT MOVE FREELY.

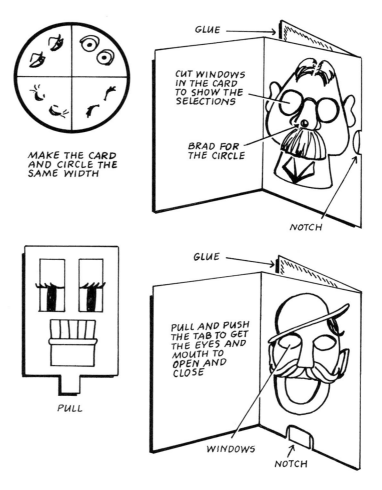

103

Pop-Up Cards

BOX FRAME

CUT THE DESIGN FROM THE WHITE PAPER, AND THE BACKGROUND FROM THE OTHER. CUT OUT THE FRAME ALONG THE SOLID LINES. SCORE AND FOLD THE DOTTED LINES. THEN GLUE ON THE SECOND PAPER.

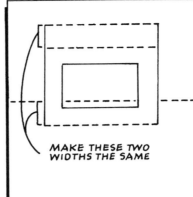

MAKE THESE TWO WIDTHS THE SAME

THIS COULD BE A PICTURE FRAME, WINDOW, OR FIREPLACE.

WORD CARD

ALIGN THE TWO PAPERS AND LAY THEM FLAT. CUT ALONG THE RIGHT AND LEFT SIDES OF THE LETTERS. SCORE A FOLD DOWN THE MIDDLE. TRIM OFF AN EDGE OR CUT A HOLE SO THE BACKGROUND IS EXPOSED.

THE CUT-OFF EDGE SHOWS THE BACKGROUND COLOR.

FLAT CARD

THIS CARD FOLDS DOWN FLAT ON THE TABLE, AND GIVES THE APPEARANCE OF A SHADOW ON EACH SIDE. CREATE MIRROR-IMAGE ART ON THE WHITE PAPER; BRIDGE THE FOLD AS SHOWN. CUT OUT THE DESIGN, EXCEPT THE BASE (DOTTED LINE). SCORE THE FOLDS AND TURN UP BOTH SIDES. GLUE THEM AT THE TOP. GLUE ON THE COLORED BACKGROUND.

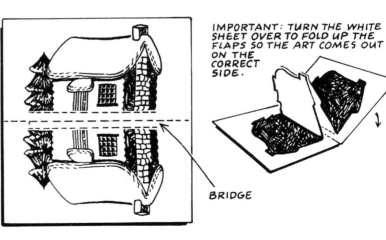

IMPORTANT: TURN THE WHITE SHEET OVER TO FOLD UP THE FLAPS SO THE ART COMES OUT ON THE CORRECT SIDE.

BRIDGE

Stand-Up Cards

FOLD LINE

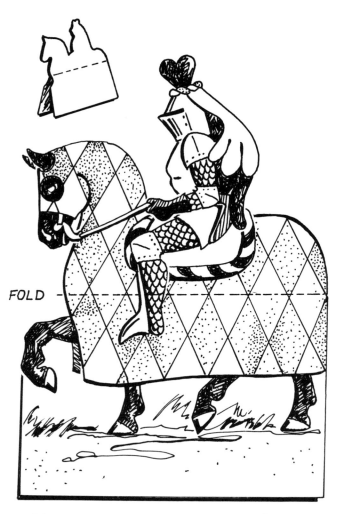

FOLD

Above: Draw the design on card stock and cut out the top half. Score the fold to the right and the left of the artwork. Turn back the top half to brace the card so it can stand up.

Above: Or cut the design from two pieces of card stock and glue them together at the top half. Score fold lines on both sides and open the card on the folds to make it stand up.

Ribbon Weaving

Weave together two or more colors of ribbon. Bond them to a backing and cut into shapes to mount on cards. Or, instead of cutting them, cut windows in the cards to frame the weaving.

SUPPLIES:

* ⅛" THICK FOAM CORE BOARD A LITTLE LARGER THAN THE FINISHED WEAVING
* TWO OR MORE COLORS OF RIBBON—A BOLT EACH
* STRAIGHT PINS
* FUSIBLE INTERFACING THE SIZE OF THE FOAM CORE
* POINTED BLACK MARKER AND RULER

1 USE RULER AND MARKER TO DRAW A 1" GRID ON THE FOAM CORE TO KEEP THE WEAVING STRAIGHT. THE FOAM CORE DOES NOT HAVE TO BE SQUARE, BUT DRAW THE LINES AT RIGHT ANGLES.

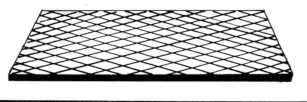

2 CUT THE FUSIBLE INTERFACING AND LAY IT, FUSIBLE SIDE UP, ON THE FOAM CORE. THE BLACK LINES WILL SHOW THROUGH. PIN THE CORNERS AS SHOWN.

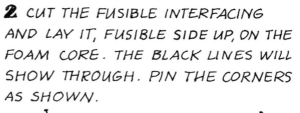

3 START WEAVING BY LAYING TWO PIECES OF RIBBON AT RIGHT ANGLES IN THE MIDDLE. FOLLOW THE GRID LINES SHOWING THROUGH THE INTERFACING. PIN THE ENDS.

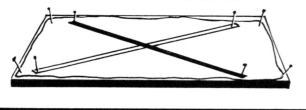

4 CONTINUE WEAVING FROM THE MIDDLE OUT. AS YOU WORK, TRANSFER THE PINS FROM THE ENDS TO THE CENTER TO KEEP THE END FREE FOR WEAVING.

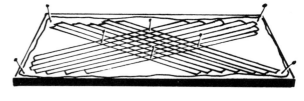
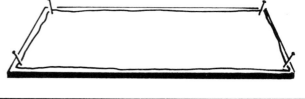

5 BY PINNING THE CORNERS OF THE MIDDLE OF THE WEAVING, THE PINS WILL BE ON THE OUTSIDE CORNERS WHEN YOU FINISH.

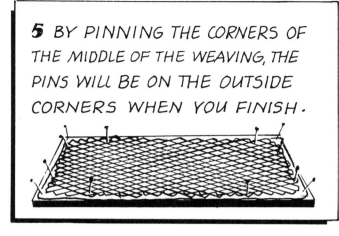

6 ADJUST THE WEAVE AND TIGHTEN IT, ONE RIBBON AT A TIME. PIN THE ENDS OF EACH ONE TO KEEP IT TIGHT.

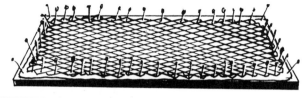

7 HEAT A STEAM IRON TO A WOOL SETTING. REMOVE THE PINS ALONG ONE EDGE AND PRESS 10 SECONDS. USE ONLY PRESSURE AND DO NOT SLIDE THE IRON AROUND.

8 ONCE THE WEAVE IS TACKED DOWN ALONG ALL EDGES, USE A PRESSING CLOTH TO IRON BOTH SIDES.

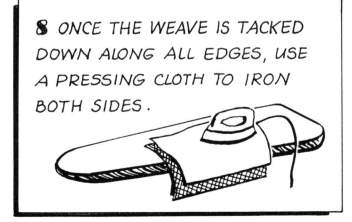

BE MINE

THIS CARD HAS THE RIBBON WEAVING SHOWING BEHIND A CUT OUT HEART FRAME.

Birthday Cake Card

USE COLORED MARKERS, GLUE, AND GLITTER TO DECORATE BOTH SIDES OF CARD STOCK. CUT OUT THE CANDLES AND THE SLIT. MAKE TWO, ONE WITH THE SLIT STARTING AT THE TOP, THE OTHER AT THE BOTTOM.

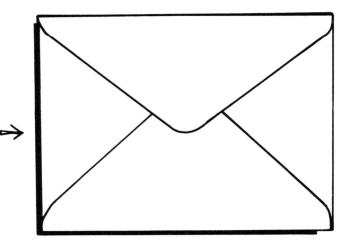

MAKE THE CARD 1/4" SMALLER THAN THE ENVELOPE.

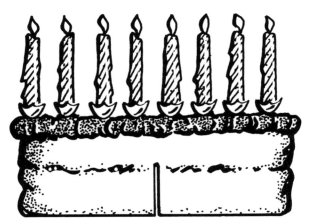

JOIN THE SLITS TO STAND UP CARD

Cut a rubber stamp that looks like a lit candle from a plastic eraser. Use it to decorate the envelope as shown here.

Color the flames with a red marker, or use glitter.

Pumpkin Card

This card is blind embossed, which means the pumpkin shape is white on a white background. the features are cut out and backed with fluorescent paper. And the pumpkin is cut out along its right edge. Use this design for Halloween, Thanksgiving, or an autumn party invitation.

CUT WHITE PAPER TO 10"X 7". SCORE AND FOLD IT IN HALF. CUT A PIECE OF FLUORESCENT PAPER TO 5"X 7".

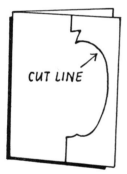

CUT LINE

NOTE: WHEN MAKING THE EMBOSSING TEMPLATE, CUT ALONG BOTH SIDES OF THE LINES ON THE PUMPKIN'S FACE TO PRESERVE THEIR WIDTHS.

Copy the pumpkin design and make it into an acetate embossing template. Emboss the cover of the card following the directions under "Embossing" on page 38. Use a sharp mat knife and cut out the eyes, nose, and mouth. Also cut out the right edge while preserving the embossed edge of the pumpkin. Put stick glue or spray adhesive on the back side of the pumpkin and back it with fluorescent paper. Letter the message inside.

Baby Announcement

This unusual card will become a family treasure. It lists five generations, and folds to fit a standard 5"x 7" envelope.

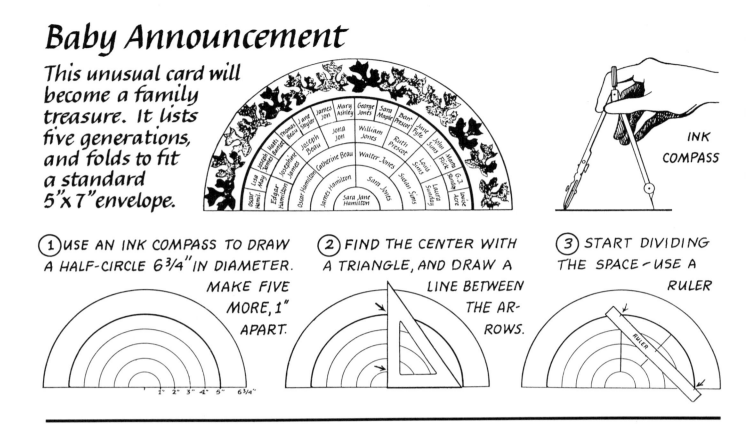

INK COMPASS

① USE AN INK COMPASS TO DRAW A HALF-CIRCLE 6¾" IN DIAMETER. MAKE FIVE MORE, 1" APART.

② FIND THE CENTER WITH A TRIANGLE, AND DRAW A LINE BETWEEN THE AR-ROWS.

③ START DIVIDING THE SPACE — USE A RULER

④ FINISH DIVIDING THE SPACE AND FILL IN THE NAMES

⑤ CUT OUT THE CARD AND DECORATE THE EDGES WITH A RUBBER STAMP THAT LOOKS LIKE A LEAF.

There's A New Leaf On Our Tree ---

⑥ SCORE VERTICAL LINES 4⅜" FROM EACH SIDE AND FOLD. DECORATE THE OUTSIDE AND ADD THE MESSAGE.

⑦ FILL IN NAME, DATE, TIME AND PLACE OF BIRTH.

⑧ DECORATE THE ENVELOPE WITH THE RUBBER STAMP.

FIRST & MIDDLE NAME

LAST NAME

DATE & TIME OF BIRTH

PLACE

110

Cards with a Map

USE THESE CARDS FOR AN OPEN HOUSE, PARTY LOCATION, OR MOVING NOTICE.

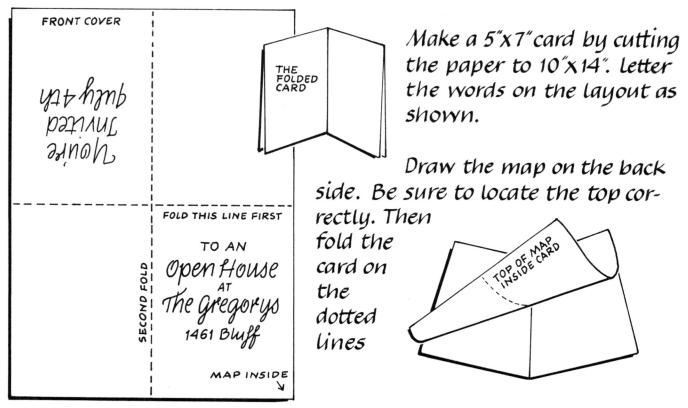

FRONT COVER

THE FOLDED CARD

You're Invited July 4th

FOLD THIS LINE FIRST

SECOND FOLD

TO AN
Open House
AT
The Gregorys
1461 Bluff

MAP INSIDE

TOP OF MAP INSIDE CARD

Make a 5"x 7" card by cutting the paper to 10"x 14". Letter the words on the layout as shown.

Draw the map on the back side. Be sure to locate the top correctly. Then fold the card on the dotted lines

Here is another map card: Cut the card to 10"x 7" and fold it in half. Letter the words on the front. Draw the map on lightweight paper that is 9 ¾"x 13 ¾". Fold it as shown and attach it inside the card with glue stick or double-sided tape. Finish lettering the words on the outside of the closed map.

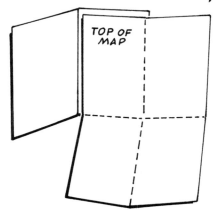

TOP OF MAP

International Cards

Use this design on cards sent to friends in other countries. Draw a stylized world map and glue a foil star where you live.

Use circles to help with the letters and their perspective.

GREETINGS FROM OHIO

Another idea is to draw the American flag and choose a star for your state.

Recipe and Coupon Cards

This card makes an inexpensive holiday gift. Cut the card so one edge folds up to make a 3"x5" recipe card with the sender's

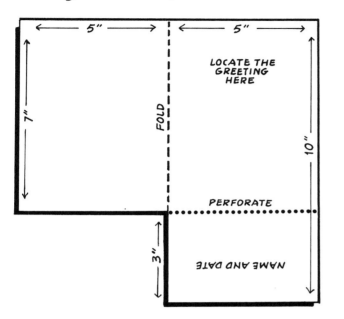

name and the date lettered upside down. Perforate the fold by running a pounce wheel along it, guided by a ruler, as shown. Fold up the card and write in a favorite holiday recipe. The 3"x5" dimensions fit a standard file

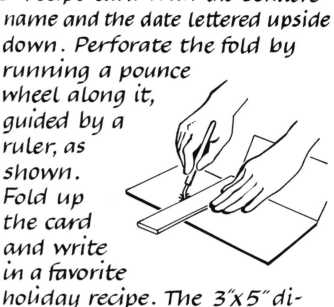

box. The name of the giver on the back will be appreciated in future years – after the recipe has become a holiday tradition.

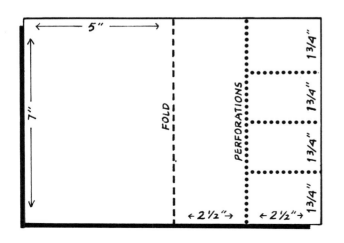

A coupon card is similar. The tear-apart coupons line up along the inside right edge. The recipient can redeem them for a compliment, an apology, a kiss, a batch of cookies, a night on the town, a phone call or visit, or anything that pleases.

Coat of Many Colors

Reward a friend at a farewell gathering, reunion, block party, retirement party, or "roast" with a card he or she will never forget.

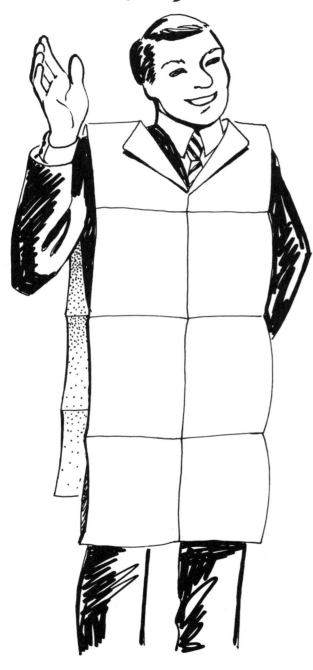

Use colored sheets of 8½" x 11" paper, and mix the colors. The coat takes 8 sheets on the front and 8 on the back. Have the person's friends write their greetings on the sheets. They can add artwork and borders, even attach photos, glitter, ribbons, candy, or money. Use markers in a variety of colors for the lettering. Decorate the sheets with rubber stamps, foil, and embossing.

Fold the four neckline sheets at front and back as shown, for a collar – and plan the decoration to fit. Tape the sheets together from the inside.

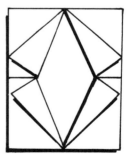

THE FOLDED NECKLINE

Game Card

Children, especially, will enjoy a greeting card that folds out into a board game. An excellent resource for games, their rules, and board designs is The Big Book of Board Games by Weinert, Beaudrot, and Palmer (Troubador Press, San Francisco, 1979). A game card serves as both greeting and gift.

SHOVE HA'PENNY

THIS IS A 16TH-CENTURY GAME LIKE SHUFFLE BOARD. TWO PLAYERS HAVE FIVE COINS APIECE. THEY SET A COIN ON THE HALF CIRCLE AND SHOVE IT ONTO THE BOARD. IF IT STOPS ON A LINE, IT DOES NOT SCORE. OTHERWISE, THE POINTS FOR EACH TOSS ARE SHOWN IN THE MARGINS. THE PLAYERS GO IN ROUNDS OF FIVE TOSSES UNTIL THE WINNER HAS LANDED A TOTAL OF THREE COINS ON EACH BAND. PILE SMALL STONES OR MATCHSTICKS IN THE MARGIN BOXES TO KEEP SCORE.

DRAW THE DESIGN ON 10"X 7" CARD STOCK, FOLDED TO MAKE A 5"X 7" CARD. MEASURE THE BANDS 1" APART. WRITE THE GREETING ON THE OTHER SIDE.

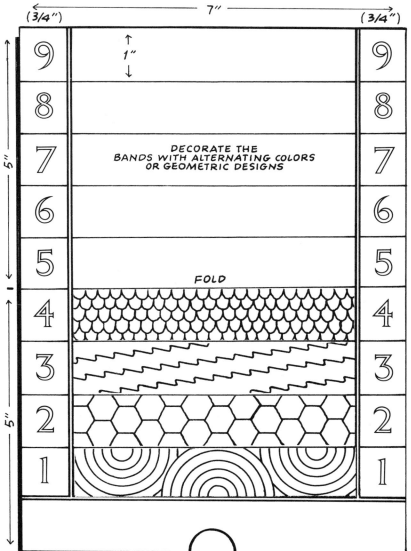

7"

(3/4") (3/4")

1"

5"

5"

DECORATE THE BANDS WITH ALTERNATING COLORS OR GEOMETRIC DESIGNS

FOLD

Stand-Up Doll Card

COPY THIS VICTORIAN LADY ONTO 8"X 10" CARD STOCK, USING THE 1" SQUARE GRID AS A GUIDE. COLOR THE DRESS WITH WATERCOLOR OR MARKERS, THEN CUT OUT THE FIGURE. LETTER THE RECIPIENT'S NAME IN THE BOX ON THE DRESS.

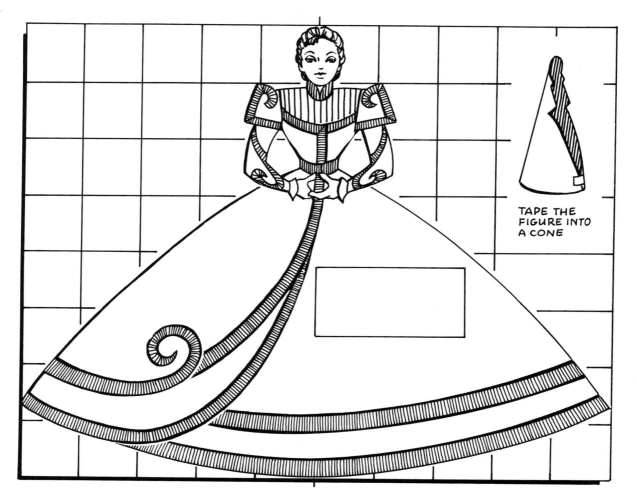

TAPE THE FIGURE INTO A CONE

CURVE BACK THE EDGES OF THE DRESS AND TAPE THEM INTO A CONE AS SHOWN. PUNCH A HOLE BETWEEN THE LADY'S HANDS AND STICK A SILK FLOWER THROUGH IT. SEND THIS CARD FLAT IN AN 8"X10" ENVELOPE. OR USE IT AS A PLACE CARD.

Photographs on Cards

A standard 3½"x5" photo goes in this card. The card fits a 5"x7" envelope.

THE COVER IS THE OUTSIDE OF SECTION B

WINDOW

WRITE GREETING HERE

¾"
¾"
¾"
¾"
1 3/8"
6 3/4"
A ← 4 5/8" →
B ← 4 3/4" →
C ← 4 3/4" →

On this card the photo is on section C behind a clear acetate window.

WRITE THE GREETING IN THE BOTTOM MARGIN.

WINDOW   WINDOW

A   B   C

Make the card from paper cut to 14 1/8" x 6 3/4" and fold as shown. Cut out a window measuring 3¼" x 4 5/8". Run double-sided tape along the opening. Center the photo and press it face down. Fold down section A and press closed.

Fold both cards the same:

C
B   A
TOP VIEW

Dimensions for this version are the same. Cut a piece of clear acetate 3½" x 5". Run double-sided tape around the window opening on section B. Center the acetate and close section A. Press. Mount the photo with double-sided tape on section C.

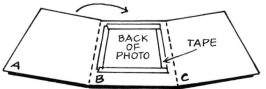

BACK OF PHOTO   TAPE
A   B   C

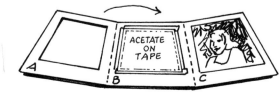

ACETATE ON TAPE
A   B   C

117

Recycled Material

MAKE ONE-OF-A-KIND CARDS FROM THE CONTENTS OF YOUR CLIP FILES. RECYCLE CATALOGS, ADVERTISEMENTS, NEWSPAPERS, MAPS, WRAPPING PAPER, AND JUNK MAIL. CUT THEM INTO COLLAGE ELEMENTS AND MOUNT THEM WITH RUBBER CEMENT OR SPRAY ADHESIVE. MAKE POSTCARDS, LINE ENVELOPES, OR CUT THEM IN A PATTERN TO MAKE ENVELOPES. IF YOU SELL OR REPRODUCE THESE IN MULTIPLES, OBTAIN PERMISSION FROM THE COPYRIGHT OWNER OF THE SOURCE MATERIAL.

Congratulations
on your new job

And you thought you couldn't bring home the bacon...

A

OPEN HOUSE

C

"Now I know why she insisted that I wear a tie."

I'm running out of ways to tell you

be MINE!

B

A. CALLIGRAPHY COMBINED WITH A MAGAZINE PHOTO MOUNTED ON CARD STOCK.

B. CHESS PIECE PHOTO FROM AN ADVERTISEMENT, AND TRANSFER LETTERS MOUNTED ON A WRAPPING PAPER BORDER.

C. THE WORDS ARE CUT FROM VARIOUS ADVERTISEMENTS AND SPRAY MOUNTED WITH OTHER ELEMENTS TAKEN FROM MAGAZINES.

D **E**

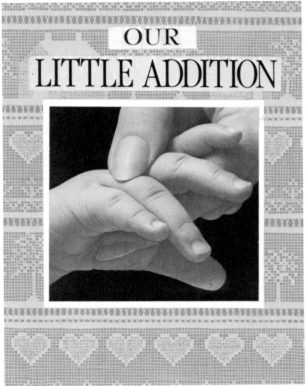

F

D. ENVELOPE MADE FROM A ROAD MAP

E. POSTCARD USING A CLIP-ART PHOTO AND PRESS-ON LETTERS MOUNTED ON CARD STOCK.

F. PHOTO AND WORDS CUT FROM A MAGAZINE AND MOUNTED ON WRAPPING PAPER

G. ENVELOPE MADE FROM A NEWSPAPER STOCK-MARKET PAGE.

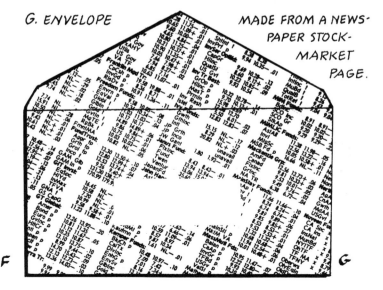

G

MISCELLANEOUS

Greeting Bag

Customize a bag to fit a gift box instead of wrapping it in the traditional manner. Write the greeting on the bag so it doubles as an original card. Choose from watercolor, glitter, foil, calligraphy, and rubber stamps to decorate your greeting bag

① Measure the circumference (c) and height (h) of the box to determine the length and width of the paper needed. Add an allowance both ways.

② Wrap the paper around the box—leave 4" to 6" extra at the top for folding down. Crease the folds.

③ Lay the paper flat again & decorate it on the lower half.

④ Wrap the box. Tape the side seam, and fold the bottom.

TUCK IN SIDES   FOLD UP BOTTOM FLAP   FOLD DOWN TOP FLAP & TAPE

⑤ Next, pinch in the sides.

Fold down the top and punch a hole to thread yarn or ribbon for a bow.

HOLE PUNCH

Or punch two holes and put a candy cane through them.

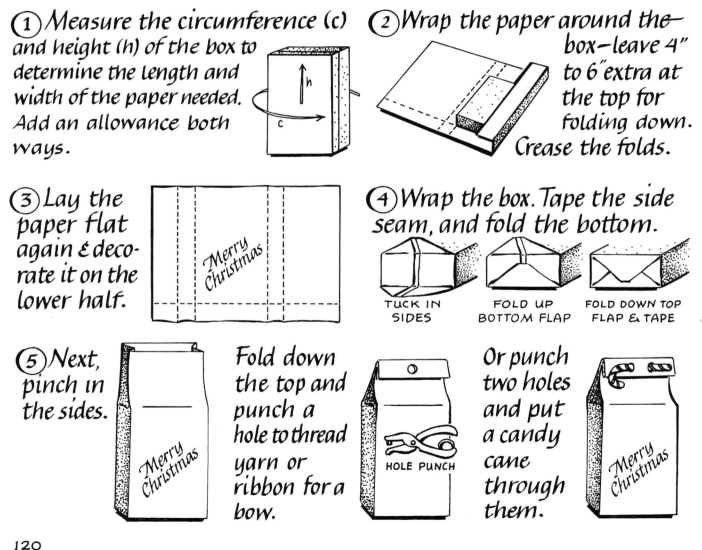

Gift Box With Handle

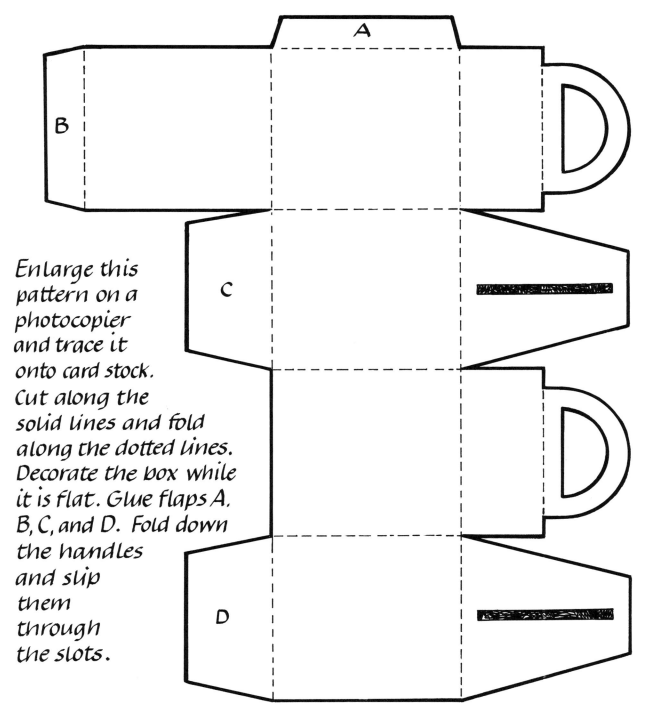

Enlarge this pattern on a photocopier and trace it onto card stock. Cut along the solid lines and fold along the dotted lines. Decorate the box while it is flat. Glue flaps A, B, C, and D. Fold down the handles and slip them through the slots.

A

B

C

D

Flat-Fold Gift Box

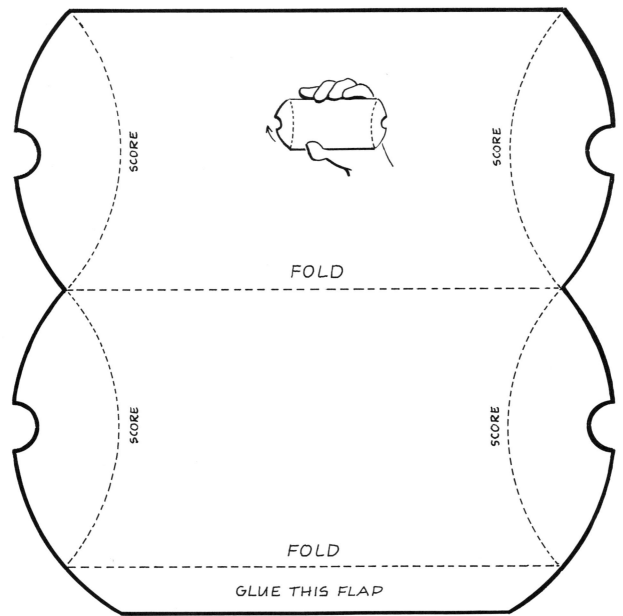

SCORE

SCORE

FOLD

SCORE

SCORE

FOLD

GLUE THIS FLAP

COPY THIS PATTERN. CUT ALONG THE SOLID LINES. SCORE THE DOTTED LINES
WITH THE POINT OF A BONE FOLDER. FOLD THE BOX IN HALF AND GLUE THE
FLAP. SQUEEZE THE BOX AS SHOWN AND FOLD DOWN THE SCORED ENDS.

Postcards

Make your own postcards from heavyweight paper and cut them to a standard size (5⅞" x 4⅛). Give them deckle, pinked, or colored edges. Mount two colored sheets, or an embossed and colored sheet for a colored edge. Make a flower collage and seal it with clear Contact® paper. Consider using a rubber stamp to outline the address area.

MARKER

TWO COLORS MOUNTED

DECKLE EDGES

← CONTACT® PAPER OVER A COLLAGE

Booklets

Use a booklet as a greeting card when you want to send a lengthy poem, relate family events, or send a special letter.

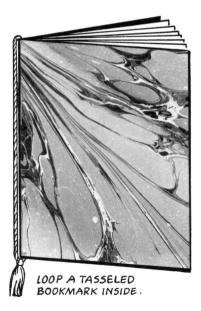

LOOP A TASSELED BOOKMARK INSIDE.

FOLD THE NUMBER OF PAGES YOU NEED IN HALF AND FLATTEN THEM WITH A BONE FOLDER. MAKE THE COVER FROM HEAVIER PAPER OF THE SAME DIMENSIONS. USE MARBLED PAPER OR DECORATE THE COVER. FOLD AND STACK THE COVER WITH THE PAGES. BIND THEM AS SHOWN ON PAGE 97. TRIM THE EDGES ACCORDING TO THE INSTRUCTIONS ON PAGE 18.

Displaying Cards

Those who make greeting cards and decorate envelopes usually collect them. Easter, Valentine's Day, birthdays, and especially Christmas are times to bring them out to display and appreciate.

Group cards according to color, material, or design. Put them on small easels to sit on fireplace mantels and desks. Hang Christmas cards on a tree by punching holes at their tops for yarn. Put the larger cards on the lower branches, and the smaller ones higher up. Attach them to a wreath, or outline a doorway, hanging them with tape.

Decorate a basket and fill it with cards for visitors to look through. Cut a door banner from felt and hang it on a dowel at the top. Add a gold cord. Sew Velcro™ strips to it, and glue Velcro™ circles to the backs of the cards to attach them. Or, instead of Velcro™, open the cards and pin them to the banner.

REFERENCE

The Business of Greeting Cards

Going into business for yourself can provide recognition for your talent and an income from doing what you enjoy — making greeting cards. You can do it full- or part-time, in a studio or in your home. Unless you have the chance to work for a card manufacturer, however, you will have to carve out a place for yourself in the market.

You already know how to make greeting cards; now you must educate yourself in such subjects as marketing, accounting, and production. Before you invest your time and your money in setting up a business, consider these questions: How is your product unique, or how does it compare to the competition? Who is your audience, and how can you reach them? Business and promotional skills cannot be overemphasized. Buy reference books or take evening or weekend classes to learn what is legally required of a small business and how to keep accurate books. Investigate the sales outlets available to you (mail order, craft shops, craft fairs, gift and stationery shops). Estimate your startup costs, which could include: permits, rent, stationery and business cards, business telephone and recorder, utilities, postage, supplies and equipment, advertising, copyright and permission fees, packaging and display costs. You may want to hire an employee, or an agent, or a sales representative. An agent or sales rep can take over the responsibility of promoting and selling your work, but you must pay a commission of 10 to 20 percent.

Since making one-of-a kind cards can keep you out of the fast lane of competition, you may want to consider using a commercial printer, who can reproduce most of the techniques described in this book from your original design. This will cut down production time and increase your output; you may be able to expand your line to include package tags, decorated envelopes, wrapping paper, and other items.

To keep down costs, you will certainly want to buy your supplies wholesale. In addition, you should take advantage of opportunities for publicity, which is free advertising: participate in craft fairs, teach through community organizations, and volunteer your skills for special events where your business name will get exposure. You should also contact local newspapers, magazines, and television stations.

BUSINESS REFERENCES

Career Opportunities in Crafts, by Elyse Sommer (New York: Crown Publishers, 1977).

The Entrepreneur's Guide to Starting A Successful Business, by James W. Halloran (New York: Liberty Hall Press, 1987).

Home Based Mail Order: A Success Guide for Entrepreneurs, by William J. Bond (New York: Liberty Hall Press, 1990).

Postal Regulations

First class postage on a greeting card mailed in the United States is a flat rate for the first ounce with a surcharge for each additional ounce. Postcards have their own rate structure. The post office has separate rates for cards mailed to Canada and to Mexico, as well as for all other international air mail.

The U.S. Postal Service regulates the size of letters and postcards it accepts because it processes mail with computerized machines. An undersized envelope cannot be mailed. An oversized postcard incurs a surcharge. The post office suggests these envelope dimensions: between 3½" and 6⅛' for height, and 5" and 11½" for width. The thickness should fall between 0.007" and 3/16". Larger envelopes are hand-processed, which slows their delivery.

The minimum size for postcards, according to postal regulations, is 3½" x 5". The maximum size is 4¼" x 6".

For envelopes, the minimum size is also 3½" x 5", but the maximum is 6⅛" x 11½".

If you need more information call your local postal service.

Hebrew Quotes for Greeting Cards

GENERAL

May peace and happiness
fill your home at this
joyous time

שלום ושמחה ישרו בביתך
בימי החדוה

Shalom

שלום

JEWISH NEW YEAR

May we be written down
in the Book of Life and
blessings for a year of
prosperity and good fortune

נכתב בספר החיים והברכות
לשנת עושר ואושר

Have a good and prosperous year

שנה טובה ומבורכת

PASSOVER

Have a happy Passover

חג פסח שמח

May the message of the
Passover remain with you
through the year

בשורת הפסח תלווה אתכם
במשך כל השנה

HANUKKAH

Have a happy Hanukkah

חג חנוכה שמח

May this holiday of joy bring
happiness to you and yours

יהי רצון שהחג יביא שמחה
לך ולבני ביתך

Symbolism of Flowers

Bluebell: Humility

Carnation: Woman's love; fascination (PINK-I WILL NEVER FORGET YOU; RED-MY HEART ACHES FOR YOU; WHITE-A WOMAN'S GOOD LUCK GIFT; SOLID COLOR-YES; STRIPED-NO, OR REGRETS)

Chrysanthemum: You are a good friend; cheerfulness (RED-I LOVE YOU; WHITE-TRUTH; YELLOW-SLIGHTED LOVE)

Daffodil: Regard; unrequited love

Daisy: Innocence; loyal love

Dandelion: Faithfulness; happiness

Forget-me-not: True love; memories

Gardenia: Secret love

Iris: Friendship; faith; hope; wisdom and valor

Ivy: Wedded love; fidelity

Jonquil: Love me; desire; sympathy

Lily: (WHITE-VIRGINITY, MAJESTY; YELLOW-I AM WALKING ON AIR; DAY LILY-CHINESE EMBLEM FOR MOTHER; TIGER-WEALTH, PRIDE; LILY OF THE VALLEY-SWEETNESS, VIRGIN MARY'S TEARS, HUMILITY)

Magnolia: Nobility

Mistletoe: Kiss me; affection

Orange Blossom: Innocence; love; marriage; fruitfulness

Poppy: Eternal sleep; imagination (RED-PLEASURE; YELLOW-WEALTH)

Rose: Happy love (CRIMSON-MOURNING; PINK-PERFECT HAPPINESS; RED-I LOVE YOU; TEA ROSE-I WILL REMEMBER; WHITE-INNOCENCE, SECRECY; YELLOW-DECREASING LOVE; BOUQUET IN FULL BLOOM-GRATITUDE; SINGLE BLOOM-I LOVE YOU)

Snapdragon: Gracious lady

Tulip: Perfect lover; fame

Traditional Jewels

January – Garnet
February – Amethyst
March – Aquamarine
April – Diamond
May – Emerald
June – Pearl

July – Ruby
August – Sardonyx
September – Sapphire
October – Opal
November – Topaz
December – Turquoise

Traditional Anniversary Gifts

YEAR
1 - Paper
2 - Calico and cotton
3 - Leather OR SIMULATED LEATHER
4 - Silk OR SIMULATED SILK
5 - Wood
6 - Iron
7 - Copper or wool
8 - Household appliance
9 - Pottery
10 - Tin or aluminum
11 - Steel

12 - Linen (TABLECLOTH, SHEETS, ETC.)
13 - Lace
14 - Ivory or bone
15 - Crystal or glass
20 - China
25 - Silver
30 - Pearls
35 - Coral or jade
40 - Ruby
45 - Sapphire
50 - Gold

Safety Precautions

There is always a risk of cuts and punctures when using scissors, mat knives, push pins, pounce wheels, and sewing needles. Handle these carefully, and store them properly. Never cut towards yourself. When you throw away a mat-knife blade or needle, tape it to a piece of cardboard first.

Keep a jar or vase near your work area to hold brushes, knives, and scissors so they are not left on the tabletop when not in use.

Wear a respirator mask if you have respiratory problems, or are concerned about harmful vapors. These include, among others, paints, solvents, adhesives, and aerosols. Avoid those that contain lead, hexane, methylene chloride, toluene, and fluorocarbons. Do not inhale metallic powders or resin.

Manufacturers will provide information on their products if you write them. Always read labels, follow suggested precautions, and store and dispose of leftover products according to their instructions.

Work in a well-ventilated, and well-lit area. Keep a first-aid kit and fire extinguisher available. Do not smoke around flammable liquids and aerosols. Do not drop hot matches or ashes into wastebaskets.

Keep art supplies out of reach of children. Supervise any project on which they work.

When working on an art project, do not handle food or rub your eyes without first washing your hands.

Do not dampen brushes with saliva, or put pens and pencils in your mouth.

Resources

Pendragon, P. O. Box 327, 14440 59th St. South, Afton MN 55001 (612-436-2046) Calligraphy and gilding

Jerry's Artarama, P.O. Box 1105, New Hyde Park, NY 11040 (1-800-827-8478) Art supplies at discount

Daniel Smith, Inc., 4130 First Avenue South, Seattle, WA 98134 (1-800-426-6740) Marbling supplies

Paper Source, 1506 West 12th Street, Los Angeles, CA 90026 (213-387-5820)

Embossing Arts, P.O. Box 626 Sweet Home, OR 97386 (503-367-3279) Thermography and stamps

Paper & Ink Books, 15309A Sixes Bridge Road, Emmitsburg, MD 21727 (301-447-6487)

Dolphin Papers, 624 East Walnut St., Indianapolis, IN 46204

Crescent Cardboard Co., 100 West Willow Rd., Wheeling, IL 60090

Strathmore Paper Co., Westfield, MA 01085

Twinrocker, P. O. Box 413, Brookston, IN 47923 Handmade paper and calligraphy supplies

Ako Shimozato, 17249 15th Ave. NW, Seattle, WA 98177 (206-546-4064) Silk-screened paper called Japanese Chiyogami

Moth Marblers, ICB Studio 345, Sausalito, CA 94965 (414-383-7213) Marbled paper

Nasco, 901 Janesville Ave., Fort Atkinson, WI 53538 (414-563-2446) Craft supplies of all types

Bibliography

Victorian Christmas Crafts by Barbara Bruno. New York: Van Nostrand Reinhold, 1987.

Christmas Trims by Better Homes and Gardens. Des Moines: Meredith Corp., 1988.

Pop-Up Gift Cards by Masahiro Chatani. Tokyo: Ondorishi Pub., LTD, 1988.

The Art and Craft of Greeting Cards by Susan Evarts. Cincinnati: North Light Books, 1975.

Greeting Cards, A Collection From Around The World by Takenbu Igarashi, editor. Tokyo: Graphic-Sha Pub, 1989.

Addressing Invitations by Joan. Monroeville, PA: Calligraphy by Joan Pub., 1990.

Creative Cards by Yoshiko Kitagawa. Tokyo and New York: Kodansha International, 1989.

The Complete Guide to Greeting Card Design by Eva Szela. Cincinnati: North Light Books, 1987.

Vogue Christmas. New York: Harper & Row, 1984.

Books, Boxes, and Portfolios by Franz Zeier. New York: Design Press, 1990.

Index